PNЯ250

VOLUME 46   NUMBER 2   NOVEMBER – DECEMBER 2019

0 Stella Halkyard Pictures from a Library   **02 PN Review** at 250
03 Editorial   **04 News** & **Notes**   **81 Gregory O'Brien** Interactions

Illustrations
Michael Augustin
(© The Artist, 2019)

CELEBRATING 250 ISSUES

'If one of the defining characteristics of most magazines is that, like most bands, they have a very short shelf life, then *PN Review* is immediately uncharacteristic. It's been going so long that many of us have all but forgotten what the P and the N stand for. I think of them as opening and closing the word Provocation. And that's why I so love the magazine.'

Paul Muldoon

'When I was at Oxford in the mid-1970s, modern poetry stopped with Auden. As Professor of Poetry, John Wain could fill the Sheldonian by lecturing on Larkin. In those pre-internet days, it was hard to find out what else was going on. The British Poetry Revival was off most people's radar. I remember standing in Blackwells and reading the newly published *North*, but it was mostly a narrow diet. Until, that is, I stumbled on *PN Review*, which began its modest, magazine-sized publication in 1976, with an issue that included Octavio Paz, Donald Davie and C.H. Sisson and led with a fighting editorial in favour of 'literary catholicity' and seriousness by Michael Schmidt. Every issue enlarged the territory (Montale, Ashbery, a review of J.H. Prynne's *Brass*), and reaffirmed Schmidt's 'belief in the centrality of the creative imagination and of... critical intelligence'. It did this not just by introducing new poets but by giving space to the half-forgotten (e.g. W.S. Graham) whose value time has endorsed.

International, venturesome, tenacious, *PN Review* has kept going by remaining true to its eclecticism and its faith in imagination and intelligence. When new issues arrive, I check out Vahni Capildeo's latest, read the editorial, then watch the whole thing open like an origami umbrella.'

John Kerrigan

'A poetry magazine can have a lifespan of a single issue or continue for more than a century, and either way leave behind a notable history; but however long they last, literary magazines do the work of discovery, and there can be no resting on laurels. That *PN Review* and Michael Schmidt – and one is inseparable from the other – have reached a landmark issue, number 250, therefore speaks literal, and enduring, volumes. Combined with the achievements of Carcanet Press, there is before us an unduplicated record of achievement; and that this has unfolded over a period of decades that have seen epochal changes not only in our world, but in poetry itself, is most remarkable. When future readers and historians alike want to see what poets were capable of in our time, they will of necessity consult the pages of *PN Review* – and when they do, they will be as intrigued and delighted as we are, its contemporary readers. What's distinctive about *PNR* is that it takes poetry and its readership seriously: it is absorbing in a way that both requires and facilitates concentration. And that's just the most salutary of its many pleasures.

On a personal note, I can say that *PN Review* has always been one of the few magazines I turn to first the moment it arrives; I tear into it, and no sooner do I finish an issue than I wander back through it, and start to wonder how soon I can see the next one. Because I know from my own work that an editor is, in a sense, only as good as the next issue, I can tell you that this ongoing momentum constitutes an enviable achievement. On an even more personal note: When I was starting out as a writer and translator of poetry, it was one of maybe three places I aspired to have work published in – and it still is.

All of which is to say that the landscape of English-language poetry is unimaginable without *PN Review*, and neither is our understanding of and appreciation for that poetry. Here's to the next 250!'

Don Share

'With its distinctive international coverage, *PN Review* is, to my mind, THE British poetry journal. I never miss an issue!'

Marjorie Perloff

Editorial

WITH THIS ISSUE *PN Review* marks its sestercentenary or, if you prefer, its semiquincentenary, or its bicenquinquagenary. As usual, the editor is on a steep learning curve, aware that we are talking 250 issues, not years.

When *PN Review* turned 200 issues old, the editorial recounted the history so far. With 250, the relief of long survival is tempered with sadness. Death has paid too many visits to the poetry world in the last two months. As I was writing this editorial, news of John Giorno's death reached us. His name joins those commemorated in News & Notes. Two losses belong in this editorial. They were of the first importance to *PN Review*. One was a co-founder of the magazine, the other a constant companion as poet, translator, essayist, reviewer and friend, from *Poetry Nation* VI (1976) to the present issue where some of her last poems are published.

Elaine Feinstein's most candid and telling prose contribution (*PNR* 224, 2015) was 'Forms of Self-Exposure', the text of a keynote lecture delivered on her behalf by Eleanor Bron at Newnham College, Cambridge, earlier that year. In a kind of life narrative, she related her experiences as woman and writer to wider contexts of world and world poetry, sharpening definitions of what she did with greater particularity in prose and interviews down the years. Her life and work unfolded in ways that enabled many writers to find vocation and 'voice'. The lecture is a summation. I like to look back to points earlier in our fifty-year friendship: we never *quite* agreed, there were the kinds of friendly resistance that led to illumination.

We shared the experience of editing magazines, and her motives as editor were not unlike mine. As an undergraduate, she edited *Cambridge Opinion*, 'an issue called "Writer out of Society", based on my enthusiasm for Ezra Pound, Samuel Beckett and Allen Ginsberg.' There was from the start an apartness in her sense of her place in relation to prevailing politics and culture. 'When I began to write I was very well aware I didn't have the right voice for current English poetry... It was partly because I was so influenced by Americans... I started my own magazine, *Prospect*, not to publish my own poems, but to introduce Olson, Paul Blackburn and others who weren't yet known in this country. That's how I came to meet Prynne. In fact, I sold *Prospect* to Prynne.' By 'sold' she meant, 'I gave him my overdraft and the title, and on that he built his connections, using my addresses... He made something much more out of them than anything I had.' The Black Mountain poets intrigued her. Olson sent her his famous letter defining breath 'prosody'.

As well as the Americans, she was alive to her family origins in the Russian-Jewish Diaspora. She developed a deep affinity with Russian poets of her century. Crucial are her translations of Marina Tsvetaeva, first published in 1971, in which she developed a 'gapped' technique to choreograph voice pauses and runs, an instinctive-seeming but deliberated Modernist technique. She translated other Russian writers and wrote biographies of Pushkin, Tsvetaeva and Akhmatova.

In her second collection, the poems are domestic, but not comfortable: instabilities, of relationship, of habitation itself. (A later poem, entitled 'Home', begins 'Where is that I wonder?') There is a tension between 'recapturing lost territory' and escaping into imagined territory. Fantasy 'encourages a steely rejection of humanism, a fashionable resistance to compassion, which I believe is as much a luxury of an English innocence as the euphoria of the affluent flower generation'. So much for the short-cut mysticisms of some of her beloved Americans. Epiphanies when they come are hard-won. I said to her in an interview in 1997, 'Risk has always been a theme with you. In 1972 you published *At the Edge*. Had I picked it up at the time I'd have thought it somehow related to Alvarez, to the edges that Alvarez talks about, but at no stage have you risked the kind of edges he advocates in the introduction to *New Poetry*.' She replied, 'I remember his introduction well. Not for me. If you've escaped the holocaust entirely by the serendipitous chance of your family deciding not to settle in Germany, and you're conscious of that – as I was from about age nine onwards – you don't look for suicidal risks much. That's not exciting. Death is not exciting.' Pressed further, she added, 'The risk I'm thinking about is the sort of risk you take in living, not playing safe.' In 'Journal' in this issue of *PN Review* she is true to the discipline of lived risk:

I remember during childbirth thinking:
well at least I can make sure this doesn't happen again,
before my first taste of a drug that allows you to cheat,
to float up to the ceiling and look down
at the hurried midwife and doctor bent over your body.

A moral, not a moralizing writer, she practices humanism in a world where poets tend to value myth and the arcana at the expense of the empirical and human. Her metonomies are not literary gestures, her images are literal and laden. She is direct with a passionate voice she found out through reading and translating Marina Tsvetaeva. Tsvetaeva 'enabled me to write without embarrassment. Because she doesn't feel embarrassed about sounding undignified'. This was a further step away from English irony towards candour. She shared her discoveries with three generations of writers. Without her, writing, especially by women, would sound different in diction, measure and tone. Without her *PN Review* would have been a different magazine.

The other loss was of James Atlas, the literary biographer and essayist, who died at the age of seventy in September. He was at Oxford on a Rhodes scholarship from Harvard when we became friends. I was developing *Poetry Nation*. He had worked on the *Harvard Advocate* and was to go on to become a notable editor (at the *New York Times*), a critic and biographer, first of Delmore Schwartz and later of Saul Bellow. *Shadow in the Garden: a biographer's tale* was published in 2017. He helped shape and temper the first issue, contributing a substantial poem and an essay on translation. He continued with us for five years, writing on Beckett, Lowell (who taught him at Harvard), and a key essay on literary biography. Without him, too, *Poetry Nation* and *PN Review* would have taken a different form.

I accompanyied him to interview the first Mrs Delmore Schwartz in London. He was working on his biography of the poet and he already knew a lot about her. She was eager to tell him that Delmore had sexual difficulties with her, which he already knew. Each time she edged towards the subject he asked distracting questions. She never got to make her revelation. Later I remonstrated with him. 'I know,' he said, 'I wasn't going to let her say it': a biographer's revenge on his subject's behalf.

His last e-mail to me, in May, ended: 'The bad news is: poor health. I just turned 70 and have a chronic lung infection, cardiovascular disease, and lots of other stuff, including gout! I don't know how long I'm going to last, but long enough to see you again, I hope. You're a dear fellow. We had fun, didn't we?' We did.

News & Notes

Ciaran Carson · *David Wheatley writes*: Ciaran Carson died on 6 October, three days short of his seventy-first birthday. He was born and died in Belfast, a city that looms monumentally over his work. Carson's father was a postman and polymath, and made Irish the language of the home; his sense of linguistic in-betweenness left an enduring mark on the future poet. A first collection, *The New Estate and Other Poems*, appeared in 1976, but it was *The Irish for No* (1987) and *Belfast Confetti* (1989) that made Carson's reputation. Their most famous poems, including 'Dresden', 'Hamlet' and 'John Ruskin in Belfast', are written in long, languorous lines that owe something to Ginsberg and C.K. Williams, but just as much to the speech rhythms of Irish storytelling or traditional *sean-nós* singing. With *Breaking News* (2003), he abruptly changed his style, espousing a staccato short line reminiscent of the Objectivists, and as also seen in *On the Night Watch* (2009) and *Until Before After* (2010). Translation was a constant, from the versions of Baudelaire, Mallarmé and Rimbaud's sonnets, in *The Alexandrine Plan* to versions of *The Táin*, Dante's *Inferno*, and Rimbaud's *Illuminations* (improbably desublimated from prose back into verse). As director of the Seamus Heaney Centre at Queen's University, Belfast, his influence on younger colleagues and students was immeasurable. In prose too he was prolific, in unclassifiable meditative works such as *The Star Factory* (1997) and *Fishing for Amber* (1999). Carson was honoured with both an Eliot Prize (1993) and a Forward Prize (2003), and deftly avoided the occasional fate of honourees of descending into a self-repeating and toothless old age. His loss has been mourned extravagantly by the Irish poetry community. A posthumous collection, *Still Life*, is a series of ekphrastic poems, summarising a life's passionate engagement with the visual world.

David Wheatley will contribute a longer appreciation to a future PN Review.

Ireland Professor of Poetry · The Irish president Michael D. Higgins announced in September that Frank Ormsby was to become the next Ireland Professor of Poetry. Ormsby follows in the distinguished footsteps of Eiléan Ní Chuilleanáin, starting at the end of October and serving until November 2022. The Ireland Chair of Poetry was estalished in 1998 when Seamus Heaney received the Nobel Prize for Literature. Ormsby declared, 'the professorship of Irish poetry is unique. It has done more than any other initiative to raise the profile of poetry in Ireland in the last 20 years, both as a recognition for established poets and a golden opportunity for younger emerging poets. The collaboration of three universities and both arts councils is a bold venture and I am honoured and thrilled to be part of it.'

John Montague was the first Ireland Professor of Poetry from 1998 to 2001 and was followed by Nuala Ní Dhomhnaill in 2001; Paul Durcan; Michael Longley; Harry Clifton; Paula Meehan; and Eilean Ní Chuilleanáin.

Nanos Valaoritis · *Evan Jones remembers the Greek poet:*
> *L'été dernier, mon ami Nanos Valaoritis a bien voulu consigner pour moi les observations qu'a appelées la trouvaille de la très belle pierre* — André Breton

The poet Nanos Valaoritis has died. Born in Lausanne, Switzerland, in 1919, he published his first poems in the mouthpiece of the Greek 'Generation of the 30s', Τα Νέα Γράμματα [*New Letters*], at the age of 18, alongside poets like George Seferis (Nobel Prize for Literature, 1963), and Odysseus Elytis (Nobel Prize for Literature, 1979). In 1944, he fled war-torn Greece and arrived in Egypt, where Seferis was in exile with the Greek government. Procuring letters of introduction to Cyril Connolly and John Lehmann, he travelled to London, where Lehmann introduced him to Stephen Spender who in turn introduced him to T.S. Eliot and Louis MacNiece. Valaoritis then found a job working with MacNiece and Dylan Thomas at the BBC on various radio programmes (he supplied any foreign accents needed). Living in London for nine years, he strengthened the relationship between Modern Greek poetry and the Anglo-Modernists; his work included the first book of translations of Seferis in English, *The King of Asine* (1948), with Bernard Spencer, and an important essay on Greek Modernism published in Connolly's magazine *Horizon* (1946).

In 1954, he moved to Paris, and there interacted with the post-war surrealist group, including André Breton, Benjamin Péret and Joyce Mansour. He returned to

Greece in the sixties, advocating the avant-garde, but his efforts were cut short by the military coup in 1967. This time, Valaoritis travelled to the US, taking a position at San Francisco State University. He taught creative writing and comparative literature there for twenty-five years, coming into contact with all of the major figures on the west coast, including Lawrence Ferlinghetti and Allen Ginsberg.

Returned to Greece in the 2000s, Nanos published – poetry, novels, studies. In 2012, his *Homer and the Alphabet*, a reading of the texts of the *Iliad* and *Odyssey* as acrophonic, Oulipian endeavours, examined in detail the correspondence between the twenty-four books of each epic and the twenty-four letters of the Greek alphabet.

I first met Nanos in the Spring of 2007. His home in Kolonaki was in an old building, with a fenced-in elevator in the foyer. He greeted me at the door of his second-floor apartment, welcomed me in and, over a cup of tea, began to talk. The details I've given above are a shortened version of the stories he told, but there were more: anecdotes about Eliot and Breton, the New Apocalyptics and *les poètes* électriques. I am not doing justice to his knowledge and interests, his humour, his limitless energy (he was eighty-six at the time and preparing a lecture on Wilhelm Reich to deliver at the University of Athens). After hours of talk, the afternoon turned into evening, I suggested I'd get going; he loaded a bag with books and joked about the 'weight of culture' as he handed it to me. That was Nanos: generous, humorous, substantial.

Menard Press turns 50 · Menard Press, which started life as a journal in 1969 with an issue devoted to Michael Hamburger, and which has been a small but fascinating producer of unexpected books of poetry and, in particular, translation, is celebrating its jubilee. In addition to literary texts – original and translated poetry, original and translated fiction, art and literary criticism – the press has published essays on the nuclear issue (by Sir Martin Ryle and Lord Zuckerman, among others) and works and testimonies by survivors of Nazism, including the first English edition of Primo Levi's poems.

Menard Press inherited F.T. Prince from Fulcrum Press in 1975; other senior poets on the list are Brian Coffey and Nicholas Moore. Translations of Nerval, Mallarmé, Rilke and Mandelstam also feature, and Sylvia Plath's translations of Ronsard and one of Elaine Feinstein's selections from the work of Marina Tsvetaeva. Menard has published studies of Charles Reznikoff, Fernando Pessoa and Primo Levi, Octavio Paz's intellectual autobiography Itinerario and Geoffrey Dutton's account of his garden in Scotland, Harvesting the Edge. Tony Rudolf has also been a close friend of *PN Review* and a regular contributor and advocate.

Al Alvarez · *Tony Roberts writes:* Al Alvarez died at the age of ninety on 23 September. A fearless critic and essayist, poet, rock climber and poker player, he seemed to thrive on a certain outsider status. From a wealthy London family of Sephardic Jews, he turned his back on the academic life, despite having gained a first in English at Oxford. Instead he took to America, to literary journalism, and then in his late twenties became a freelance writer.

Having proved an influential poetry editor for the *Observer* (1956-1966), Alvarez extended his reputation with the *Penguin Modern European Poets* series, from 1967. Over the years there followed at least twenty non-fiction books, including the provocative anthology *The New Poetry* (1962) and the cult classic, *The Savage God: A Study of Suicide* (1972).

Although Alvarez encouraged the early work of Gunn, Hill, Hughes, Plath, Porter and others; his anthology, *The New Poetry*, scandalised. There he championed Lowell, Berryman, Sexton and Plath as a snub to the 'gentility' of British verse, which he later wrote 'didn't seem an adequate response to a century that had spawned two world wars, totalitarianism, genocide, concentration camps and nuclear warfare' (*Where Did It All Go Right?*).

Also problematic was the controversy over *The Savage God*, a book which explored cultural attitudes to suicide, opening with a long detailed piece on Plath's. Hughes responded furiously and, though Alvarez was to point out that he had neither sensationalised nor criticised Plath, the account was inevitably intrusive.

Alvarez admired American poetry, asserting that 'modernism has been predominantly an American concern' (*The Shaping Spirit*). He felt indebted to the country, revelling in the energy he found at Princeton, where he delivered the Gauss Seminars in 1958. His admiration for poetry 'on the friable edge between the tolerable and intolerable' (*The Writer's Voice*) led Alvarez to champion European poetry, particularly that written under the most Orwellian circumstances.

He was later to tone down his position on risk. In a piece for *The New York Times* in 1972 – after Berryman's suicide – he wrote, 'For years I have been extolling the virtues of what I have called extremist poetry, in which the artists deliberately push their perceptions to the very edge of the tolerable. Both Berryman and Sylvia Plath were masters of the style. But knowing now how they both died I no longer believe that any art – even that as fine as they produced at their best – is worth the terrible cost.'

A highly talented and independent spirit, Al will be missed.

'A Poem against Injustice and Corruption' and its consequences · Radio Farda reported on 6 October that 'a poetry reciter' (presumably a performance poet using traditional verse forms, and also a 'sonneteer') in Iran was sentenced to six months in prison for performing a 'poem against injustice and corruption, discrimination, abusing power and stealing public funds'. Hossein Jannati was not unknwn to the establishment, having performed before Iran's Supreme Leader Ali Khamenei in the past. He has been charged with 'propaganda against the regime', and a higher court confirmed the verdict on 5 October. Posting on Instagram, Jannati was unrepentant. He declared he would not be silenced on issues of 'oppression, injustice, abuse of power and religion'. The verdict related to a recital at the university of Isfahan.

On Instagram he recalled that his father consoled him: 'God is greater than the Sultan.'

Günter Kunert (1929–2019) · *Michael Augustin writes*: I wouldn't be able to say how often during the past thirty years or so poor Günter Kunert saw himself confronted with my Radio Bremen microphone, how often he happily read brand new poems for my various literature programmes and how often I had the unbelievable pleasure of drawing from the overflowing barrel of his personal memories.

The son of a Jewish mother and a non-Jewish father, Günter Kunert had survived the holocaust in the inner city of Berlin while many in his family were deported and murdered in the German concentration camps. After the Hitler years he stayed on to live and write in the Eastern part of the city. Two writers who couldn't possibly represent more opposite characters – Johannes R. Becher and Bert Brecht – were charmed by young Kunert and did what they could to help him make a start as a writer.

After he and his first wife Marianne, accompanied by seven cats, had turned their backs on repressive East Germany in 1979 the couple settled in an old former school-house right in the middle of nowhere – in Kaisborstel, way up in the countryside of Schleswig-Holstein. He simply wanted to live without neighbours after years of Stasi scrutiny and twenty-four-hour surveillance. The big city had become too suffocating for the free spirit he was. From now on he would look across a field all the way to the horizon when sitting at his desk: nulla dies sine linea!

One thing which always fascinated me about Günter was his stunning ability to combine melancholia with humour. His humour, I believe, served him as a bullet-proof vest, which throughout his life allowed him to fire back at his many adversaries. Wolf Biermann once called him a 'jolly pessimystic' (sic!) which sounds far more accurate to me than 'The Kassandra of Kaisborstel', another label stuck on him (which he truly seemed to enjoy) due to his sceptical view of the world and his fellow humans. He had no illusions about mankind which he always saw in the process of going down the drain. Good to know we have his poems – something to cling on to as the flood rises.

The Scottish Poetry Library in crisis · Those of us who have loved the Scottish Poetry Library in Edinburgh have been appalled at the recent controversy surrounding its management. Four honorary presidents, the former Scots Makar Liz Lochhead, Douglas Dunn, Michael Longley and Aonghas MacNeacail, resigned in a joint letter saying they were 'deeply unhappy' with its current management and governance. Former staff have added their voices to the growing protest at the regime of the current director and the 'toxic work environment' that has overtaken what was a happy and well-run Scottish national resource. Thirteen members of staff (and it is a small, specialized staff) have resigned since the appointment of the current director Asif Khan three years ago. This 100% turnover has been described as 'disastrous and wholly indicative of systemic management failures'. The former employees felt 'obliged to speak out to preserve the SPL's reputation and future'. Their concern is not new: one year after Khan's appointment twenty of Scotland's leading poets expressed concern about the library's hierarchy and described it as a 'scene of unhappiness'. Jackie Kay, the current Scots Makar, and Carol Ann Duffy were among signatories of a letter expressing a 'real sense of concern'

about the library's direction and management. It was set up in 1984 and moved into handsome purpose-built premises near the Scottish Parliament twenty years ago.

Michael Mott · *Just as* PN Review 250 *was going to press, Tony Roberts wrote:* Michael Mott, who has died at 89 in Decatur, Georgia, was a distinguished poet, biographer and novelist (as well as an inveterate raconteur and gracious host).

Born in London, Michael's father was an English solicitor, his mother a sculptor from Denver, Colorado. He moved to America in 1966 to act as poetry editor of the Kenyon Review. A Guggenheim Fellow, Michael was twice Writer-in-Residence at The College of William and Mary in Virginia. He completed a best-selling biography, *The Seven Mountains of Thomas Merton*, before retiring from teaching in 1992.

Michael won the Allen Tate Prize in Poetry in 2002 and, over the years, published eleven collections of poetry, including the prize-winning *The World of Richard Dadd* (2005).

The two-headed Nobel Prize · On 10 October the Polish novelist Olga Tokarczuk and the Austrian writer Peter Handke were announced as recipients of the Nobel Prize for Literature for 2018 and 2019 respectively. The 2018 decision was delayed after a sexual scandal and the resignation of the Swedish selection committee. That scandal has been displaced by another.

Tokarczuk's award seemed unexceptional: the novelist is clearly a substantial figure and the relative unfamiliarity of her *oeuvre* in Anglophone countries was more a judgement on them than on the selectors. The Academy celebrated Tokarczuk 'for a narrative imagination that with encyclopedic passion represents the crossing of boundaries as a form of life'.

On the other hand, the selection of Peter Handke set in train an entirely new scandal. Handke, the Academy declared, received the award 'for an influential work that with linguistic ingenuity has explored the periphery and the specificity of human experience'. Many authors were quick to condemn the selection. Salman Rushdie, Hari Kunzru and Miha Mazzin were prompt to voice their alarm. In 1999 Rushdie chose Handke as runner-up for 'International moron of the year' for his 'series of impassioned apologias for the genocidal regime of Slobodan Milošević'. Handke attended and spoke at Milošević's funeral in 2006.

His debut with a novel and a play was in 1966. 'More than fifty years later, having produced a great number of works in different genres, 2019 Literature Laureate Peter Handke has established himself as one of the most influential writers in Europe after the Second World War,' the Academy announced. 'The peculiar art of Peter Handke is the extraordinary attention to landscapes and the material presence of the world, which has made cinema and painting two of his greatest sources of inspiration.'

The President of American PEN said she and the body over which she presides were 'dumbfounded' by the award to 'a writer who has used his public voice to undercut historical truth and offer public succour to perpetrators of genocide, like former Serbian President Slobodan Milošević and Bosnian Serb leader Radovan Karadzic. We reject the decision that a writer who has persistently called into question thoroughly documented war crimes deserves to be celebrated for his "linguistic ingenuity". At a moment of rising nationalism, autocratic leadership, and widespread disinformation around the world, the literary community deserves better than this. We deeply regret the Nobel Committee on Literature's choice.'

As *PN Review 250* went to press, German PEN had yet to make a statement. There is no Günter Grass to turn to for a decisive judgement on the judgement.

Etheridge Knight · *Jim Kates writes:* The Indianapolis poet Jared Carter introduced Etheridge Knight to me – or, more accurately, passed Knight along. Etheridge was a brilliant poet, a delightful companion, and an exuberant, unapologetic freeloader. He stayed with me in Jaffrey, New Hampshire, several times while he taught at the nearby Dublin School and participated in rehabilitation at a nearby facility, Beech Hill. From time to time his lover, Liz McKim, came out from Boston to join us.

Etheridge and I had northern Mississippi in common. He was originally from Corinth, while I had spent time in Panola County. He claimed I made the best grits he had ever tasted. 'I just follow the instructions on the box,' I told him. Those winter days, Mississippi felt far away.

Jaffrey then was a very white New Hampshire town still dealing with Klan recruitment – I'd had a small fire-bomb set off at my house when I'd moved in a few years earlier. One January day Knight went out for a walk – and he came back all excited:

'Jim, the Challenger exploded!'

'How do you know?' I asked.

'A man came up to me on the street and told me.'

My first reaction: 'A strange white man spoke to you on the street?!!' That was more newsworthy to us than the shuttle disaster.

Etheridge had struggled with addiction ever since his military service in Korea. When I wasn't looking, he emptied my liquor cabinet, down to the sweet liqueurs. But he was never, in my presence, visibly drunk or otherwise impaired, and it wasn't something we mentioned explicitly.

When he wasn't staying with me, we sometimes talked by telephone:

Me: 'Eth, how you doing?'

Him: 'Fine, man, eleven days now, eleven days!'

Me: 'So, how are you?'

Him: 'Thirteen days – thirteen days! Going well.'

Me: 'How are you?

Him: 'Fine.'

What we conversed about together was poetry. One of his most brilliant poems, 'Ilu, the Talking Drum', intersected with my own experience of learning about African drumming at Wesleyan University. He delighted also in the impromptu discipne of haiku/senryu. I don't have any of his at hand (I think he published some of these) but I do have a couple of my own contributions to the mix, and they resonate for me in our common language:

Stove cold. Two days' news
to get it sucking again.
Thank you, Mr. Bush.

You ask how I am.
I say my most recent poem
and ask how are you.

Etheridge left me with a handsome broadside of one of his most beautiful and heartfelt poems, 'Circling the Daughter'. It had an error in it. The line, 'A flower is moral by its own flowering' had been misprinted 'A flower is mortal by its own flowering' and – against my protest – he struck out the 't' by hand. The poem resonated with both readings.

The last I saw Knight, he had risen from a hospital bed to participate in a benefit reading with Robert Bly and Sharon Olds at Sanders Theatre, Cambridge. Etheridge didn't like to say he 'read' poems, he always talked about 'saying' them; and, with his first recitation, he brought down the house. Every 'saying' was followed by enthusiastic applause. Bly, who followed Knight in the program, was clearly upset that his own poems were not similarly appreciated, but met the usual polite silence of a reading.

A poem I had written for Knight ('Letter to Etheridge') turned out to be valediction after his death in March 1991, although not intended as such:

Your black drumbeats no longer stretch these white yankee
    walls.
In the upstairs room your smoke hangs in the air
as if you'd been Old Scratch on a business trip
breathing in and breathing out, leaving a brimstone
    souvenir
straight from the belly, or carrying it like riding dust
clung to your accustomed clothing
and shook down.

You took the electric heater, good,
and a pair of warm winter boots
abandoned by a former tenant
who made his own bargain with this climate.
He's married now, a place of his own under the sun,
a fine car, and all the grits he can eat –
except he don't eat grits.

You travel light enough to fly, brother.
You left your summer duds in collateral,
secure as far as I'm concerned from barter
(even those shoes that pinch your wide feet)
until you settle.
They're here, safe as houses.
And I've still got my soul

and a bottle of good Irish whiskey.
There are some devils loose in the world
the whippoorwill can't whistle away.
Mr. Miles writes from Mississippi:
he made his crop but still might lose his farm.
In the long war between cold and warm,
cold is winning.

Harold Bloom · *Andrew Latimer writes:* 'You must choose. Either there are aesthetic values or there are only the overdeterminations of race, class and gender.' One cannot have one's cake and subvert it, argued Harold Bloom, the eminent American literary critic, who has died aged eighty-nine. Bloom, the author of more than forty works of criticism, will be remembered, somewhat patronisingly, as a larger-than-life Johnsonian character who was known to devour whole novels in one hour and propound absolute truths from 'The Chair', the well-filled seat from which he occupied an increasingly elevated yet tenuous teaching position at Yale University. Above all, he will be remembered as *divisive*. His reputation as a controversialist, established in the 1973 study of poetic agons, *The Anxiety of Influence: A Poetic Theory*, was cemented with *The Western Canon: The Books and School of Ages* (1994). Bloom's canon was condemned as an 'act of ethnic and sexist oppression' by his critics – those he termed the School of Resentment. Though he remained unapologetic about the book's argument, he did express regret at having appended a list of canonical works to *The Western Canon* at the publisher's behest. Such a list reduced Bloom's canon to a prescriptive list of stable, distinct works; but at its heart, it is a record of interconnected creative acts of literary genius. Choosing which to pursue and which to ignore is not only vital to the work of literary criticism, he argued, it is also a part of that creativity. 'You must choose', and whether we choose to continue to engage with Bloom or not, his legacy remains, first and foremost, one of humanity – with Shakespeare at its core: 'Bloom isn't asking us to worship great books,' wrote Adam Begley in *The New York Times*, 'he asks instead that we prize the astonishing mystery of creative genius.'

David Rosenberg will contribute an essay on Harold Bloom and his legacy to a future issue of PN Review.

'Recent Poetry' © Michael Augustin

Even You Song

The Boisterous Weeping of Margery Kempe

VAHNI CAPILDEO

Could you imagine going on a mission to the moon with your partner? Writer Lucy Sheerman and artist Bettina Furnée interviewed a series of couples, asking them just that. The couples' responses, and images from their ordinary home life, intercut with thoughts on the Apollo missions and moon landing, were transformed into a new Evensong. Cheryl Frances-Hoad's musical setting, while singable by a good community choir, moves rapidly between unusual time signatures and keys, providing a stretch and stress of shimmer and rest for the libretto. The premiere of *Even You Song* took place at Peterborough Cathedral on 16 February 2017, as a collaboration with Metal Culture, Peterborough. There will be further performances, including one at St James's, Piccadilly, on 29 November 2019.[1]

Each performance has unique elements. Sheerman and Furnée have invited different writers to provide, and if possible perform, short reflections as part of this ongoing project. I was thrilled and terrified to be invited to take responsibility for the reflection on 15 July 2019, the fiftieth anniversary of the moon landing. On that occasion, the historic Kings Lynn Minster, with its tidal moon clock and tide highwater marks at the western door, was the location for *Even You Song*. Kings Lynn is famously associated with the fifteenth-century mystic and unruly voyager, Margery Kempe. I went into deep retreat for a week, reading her Life in the original. Here is the result.

'Going to the moon is extreme.

"But no," a confident traveller might say. "You can choose many pathways to the moon, even when it's far in its elliptical orbit. The first men on the moon needed less than half a week from lift-off to landing. It can take almost as long to find connecting flights from Britain to the east of Iceland. Going to the moon isn't extreme."

"Only three or four days to the moon! That is exactly what is extreme," their friend might answer, hiding their own wish to visit the moon. "So suddenly to be in a place where you can leave footprints but not fingerprints; where touch is gloved, and every breath you draw is a breath that depends on something."

Every breath you draw is a breath that depends on something.

Here is something to explore. When you are in outer space, beyond the bluegreen marble, among the stars, with just one other person, depending on each other, far out and feeling as if it's forever, how do you have space? Inside your head? What is happening to the space inside your head? Where is your you-time? How do you not lose yourself?

"I've been travelling so long," the confident traveller said, "that I've learnt to tune in to the sounds around me and blank them out like white noise. A motorway, the seaside, workers going up and down a scaffold, school at break time, town on a Friday night? I stay sane by blending sound into a safe blur, using my own resources. Not headphones. Tune in and blank out."

"But on the way to the moon? How can you blank out knowing you are in space?" asked the secretly hopeful traveller.

And the confident traveller said, "I tune in to the memory of sounds, or even to imaginary ones. I could tune into space itself. Imagine oscillating between vast silence and eerie waves. Totally blank out the person I am with, to stay together."

"Oh," said their friend, afraid of being cancelled. They began to practise having imaginary conversations with themselves, visualising fantasy gardens, and choosing ideal pets. This way they would have inner resources when they left everything behind for their interstellar voyage, in which from time to time over a very long time they would naturally find themselves separate, or need separation, from the other person who was bodily present.

To be quick to comfort a loved one in distress, but to lose patience if the distress continues, and walk away from the nagging of sadness, the tedium of trauma, may be possible if you are mobile and in the same space, but not if you are literally in space together.

You know the way some sports are classed as 'extreme sports'? Your companion to the moon is your extreme neighbour. For an extreme neighbour, extreme empathy...

Five hundred years ago in Kings Lynn lived a woman named Margery Kempe. The book of her life is often treated as a story of extremes, because she would burst out weeping in public, sometimes softly like small drops of rain, frequently roaring tempestuously. Her crying and sobbing was plentiful, described as boisterous.

What would you do if at Evensong, in the dignified premises of a beautifully maintained building, the person next to you collapsed in a fit of emotion, with the invasion of your own space that would bring, by sound, by convulsive movement, by bodily fluids? What if your travelling-companion to the moon behaved like that? In the company of an extreme neighbour, could you meet the challenge of extreme empathy? What if you were the one irresistibly overcome?

Both in her home town, and on her journeys, where she did not have modern communications or transport, Margery Kempe was abandoned, bad-mouthed, stolen from, sent away, threatened with assault and death; forced to account for herself to the authorities. Was Margery Kempe too much? Excessive? But who is excessive, where is excess, in her book? Isn't the hostility people showed to this embarrassing fountain of tears also excessive in word and deed, violence and neglect?

Perhaps to be moved by the desire to go to the moon can be understood figuratively. Perhaps, going to the moon, you test your systems as if you were a lunar-bound device. Perhaps going to the moon is going beyond the boundaries of what 'normal society' expects, and overturning the boundaries of a beautifully maintained self.

Margery Kempe's outpourings sometimes met with kinder responses. Sometimes people suffered her patiently. Suffering, not putting up with; not keeping calm and carrying on. Suffering, going through an experience with someone strange to yourself. Not pretending to feel the

---

1 https://www.ticketor.com/londonoriana/event/even-you-song-169586.

same, but admitting and allowing yourself to be affected. Weeping as an unsealing of the closed self, not only the weeper's self, but the neighbour's. Not duress, but endurance. Not tuning out, but sharing time. Durational listening. Rupture. Rapture.

When the confident traveller's confidence cracks, who is their companion? Do they crack and let in the unbreathable atmosphere of fear? Or make another vital system fire up, in the acceptance of how things are?

In Margery Kempe's life, some people listened with delight to her when she was able to speak. Light is known by contrast and kinship with darkness. Earth and water are palpably different from each other, though similar in both being unstable and stable, supporting houses or bearing up ships, while yet being subject to earthquakes, erosion and tides. So the value of silence, and going within yourself to think, becomes better known by contrast and in phases. Silence and rest are cherished, and even fulfilled, by being neighbours to uncontainable feelings and expressions.

Although Margery Kempe was moved by the love of Christ, it is not necessary to have a textbook belief to appreciate that His story offers itself as embodying all human potentiality. Margery Kempe's self-abandonment arose in her passionate hyperconsciousness of Christ, from tiny things, such as the mere fact of being born and being a child (sometimes she wept at the sight of a child in the street), to the extremes of protest, interventions, doubt, torture and sacrifice, which she was willing to contemplate and undertake in her own life.

When this text was read in Kings Lynn, Margery Kempe of five hundred years ago was present as our neighbour in place. She is also our neighbour in time. Her vivid and personal relationship to the story of Christ, as if it were ongoing in her own life, is a model of how to live two stories at once. She let go of her husband, fourteen children and safety as a woman in the Middle Ages, to go as and where she felt she must, in continual relationship with her vision. Thus excess is a phase of normality. Disruption of a service triggers the fulfilment of the service, intensifying people's involvement.

Going to the moon is extreme; and yet, and therefore, has its part of human ordinariness, also co-extensive with earthly life.'

Plum and Porter

WILLIAM POULOS

In the early twentieth century, musical theatre on Broadway was as American as apple strudel. Producing shows about Parisian hatters and Viennese milkmaids singing waltzes and gypsy songs, Broadway needed someone to write stories and lyrics that were quintessentially American. Further proof that the United States of America is the greatest product of the British Empire, the man to do this was P.G. Wodehouse.

As the theatre critic for *Vanity Fair*, Wodehouse saw a show composed by Jerome Kern, who had already given Broadway a musical facelift. Complaining about the poor lyrics, Wodehouse was hired as Kern's new lyricist, and with Guy Bolton the trio produced their shows at the Princess Theatre. The 'Princess Theatre' style was instantly successful; in 1918 Dorothy Parker, Wodehouse's successor at *Vanity Fair*, wrote: 'Bolton and Wodehouse and Kern are my favourite indoor sport. I like the way they go about a musical comedy... I like the way the action slides casually into the songs.' Eschewing the euphemisms and puns of the Hapsburg-influenced lyricists, Wodehouse deftly played with American vernacular. Here are his lyrics about Cleopatra from the 1917 Bolton-Wodehouse-Kern show *Leave it to Jane*:

She gave those poor Egyptian ginks
Something else to watch besides the sphinx

From these two lines you quickly learn what a 'gink' is, how dull life must be for one, and how seeing a beauty like Cleopatra would liven things up. All good songwriters have this talent for economy because they know they must get all the information across at once; the audience can't ask the singer to repeat a line. Later in the song, Wodehouse describes Cleopatra's ability to make men swoon permanently:

When out with Cleopatterer
Men always made their wills.
They knew they had no time to waste
When the gumbo had that funny taste.
They'd take her hand and squeeze it
They'd murmur 'Oh, you kid!'
But they never liked to start to feed
Till Cleopatterer did.

With comic and technical facility like this (how many songwriters can handle a double infinitive so easily?) it's no wonder that Wodehouse became the exemplary American lyricist, with Ira Gershwin, Oscar Hammerstein II, Lorenz Hart and Cole Porter all following his lead.

Wodehouse worked with both Gershwin and Porter. Wodehouse and Bolton wrote the book for Porter's show *Anything Goes* and retained the credit after substantial revision by Crouse and Lindsay. Even thirty years after the show opened, Wodehouse complained about Porter's lyrics, writing that the 'poor devil' became exhausted after five refrains. In a letter to Ira Gershwin, Wodehouse scolds Porter for 'bunging anything down' and not making sense, quoting this verse from 'Anything Goes':

When Mrs R. with all her trimmins
Can broadcast a bed by Simmons,
Then Franklin knows
Anything goes

'What the hell does "trimmins" mean?' Wodehouse asks Gershwin. I'm not down with American slang, but surely it means 'accessories'? (You might fairly ask 'what the hell does "broadcast a bed" mean?', but this refers to the broadcasts Eleanor Roosevelt made for the Simmons

Mattress Company.) In a letter to Guy Bolton at around the same time, Wodehouse asks what Porter's lyric 'you're Inferno's Dante' means and says that Porter's readiness to rhyme anything shows a dangerous lack of self-criticism. He offers a revised verse:

> When the courts decide, as they did latterly
> We could read Lady Chatterly
> If we chose,
> Anything goes

And says it's 'a darned sight better than anything old King Cole ever wrote'. I think that Wodehouse is too critical of Porter – Wodehouse himself wasn't immune to the temptation of writing a word just because it rhymed. In the song 'It's a Hard Hard World for a Man' he wrote:

> The history books are full of tales
> Of fellows who were perfect whales
> At virtue when they started their career.

What does it mean to be a 'perfect whale at virtue'? In a revised version of 'You're The Top' there's another dubious rhyme. Porter's original lyrics compare a lover to eminent things in the world. For example:

> You're the nimble tread of the feet of Fred Astaire
> You're an O'Neill drama,
> You're Whistler's mama,
> You're camembert.

This verse became:

> You're Mussolini
> You're Mrs Sweeny
> You're Camembert.

I'm not sure what this means either. Is Mussolini the top? If he's the top, who's the bottom?

Things get a bit tricky here, especially considering Wodehouse's infamous Berlin broadcasts. Wodehouse revised Porter's lyrics for London, but there's little good evidence he wrote these lines. (There's no evidence suggesting Porter wrote them). At this time, too, Wodehouse was writing *The Code of the Woosters*, in which he created the immortal Sir Roderick Spode, leader of the Black Shorts. Anyone who thinks that Wodehouse had fascist sympathies should reread this exchange between Bertie and Gussie:

> 'By the way, when you say "shorts", you mean "shirts", surely?'
> 'No. By the time Spode formed his association, there were no shirts left. He and his adherents wear black shorts.'
> 'Footer [football] bags, you mean?'
> 'Yes.'
> 'How perfectly foul.'

Wodehouse deflates the pretensions of Spode, who is a fat, bald bully with a jutting chin (who does that sound like?) by revealing his secret profession as a designer of ladies' underwear. As Bertie says: 'You can't be a successful Dictator and design women's underclothing. One thing or the other. Not both.' Wodehouse used his comic invention to topple fascists, not exalt them.

Comedy wasn't his only talent. He wrote the lyrics for the melancholy ballad 'Bill', which became the most famous song from *Show Boat*. Abandoned by her husband, the despondent Julie describes an imperfect lover:

> I used to dream that I would discover
> The perfect lover someday...
> His form and face
> His manly grace
> Are not the kind that you
> Would find in a statue...
> And I can't explain,
> It's surely not his brain
> That makes me thrill –
> I love him because he's wonderful,
> Because he's just my Bill.

Wodehouse's friend and disciple Ira Gershwin imitated this sentiment and trick of spreading a rhyme over two words in his own ballad 'Someone to Watch over Me', in which the lonely Kay despairs of ever finding affection:

> Looking everywhere, haven't found him yet
> He's the big affair I cannot forget
> Only man I ever think of with regret...
> Although he may not be the man some
> Girls think of as handsome
> To my heart he carries the key.

Gershwin and Wodehouse admired each other, and the two kept in contact throughout their lives. In his preface to the song 'Things Are Looking Up', Ira wrote that it's to be sung 'on the downs of Totleigh Castle, located in Upper Pelham-Grenville Wodehouse, England'. Cole Porter's thoughts are not recorded.

Letter from Wales

Sam Adams

We are becoming accustomed to assertions in public life that are less than the whole truth and all too often downright lies. In literature we meet, increasingly it seems, narrative fiction based on skeletal fact, as well as work planned and presented to deceive, like Macpherson's Ossian, Chatterton's Rowley poems and Iolo Morganwg's masterly imitations of Dafydd ap Gwilym, as previously mentioned (*PNR* 249). While searching for a reference I knew to be found in Rhys Davies's *Print of a Hare's Foot*, I was so charmed, once again, by the stories and their telling that I re-read the whole book. It comes into the category of unreliable memoirs, its primary function to entertain rather than factually inform. Davies termed it 'An Autobiographical Beginning', raising expectations of a forthcoming middle and (near) end. But there was no more, for he was nearing the end of a productive and successful writing career, and what we have is filled out with pieces previously published in Geoffrey Grigson's miscellany *The Mint* and Connolly's *Horizon*.

The book begins with a Proustian moment, not a madeleine dipped in tea, but the finger touch of a 'a roll of vividly striped flannel' of the 'old hairy breed' on a stall at Carmarthen market. It brings back the horror of Sunday's fresh-laundered flannel shirt following the weekly bath, the essential preliminary to morning service at Gosen, the tiny Congregational chapel not far from his parents' grocery shop: 'Seated alone in my mother's rented pew... I scarcely dared move within my hairshirt. To rise for hymn-singing renewed the hot itching of my miserable flesh. [The Minister] Mr Walters's demoniac preaching, mounting into *hwyl* sometimes, brought forgetfulness. A good exponent of this chanting eloquence, he roared, thumped the pulpit-ledge, pointed an accusing finger at nastinesses among us, thundered our guilt. He placed a solid load of this mysterious guilt on my back, and I was suitably shirted to receive it.' And he is transported back to historical characters and events and 'Children's Games'.

I am half-inclined to believe this caricature of the Welsh chapel composed for the amusement of English readers. The chapel, or at least the building that once was Gosen, stands near the corner where Thomas Street joins Jones Street, and Mr Walters was my wife's great-uncle. She has no recollection of him, but as a child she took her turn, after elder sisters' strenuous objections had finally obtained them relief from the duty, as overnight companion to her widowed great-aunt, in case she passed away in her sleep. In the candlelit spare bedroom of the gloomy house, desperate for print, she read the yellowed newspapers that lined the drawers of a haughty chest. But how do you square Davies's description of morning service and a sermon in Welsh with what we certainly know from his brother Lewis's testimony: a family connection with St Thomas's, a church even nearer to 'Royal Stores', was strong enough for him to harbour a youthful ambition to train for the Anglican priesthood.

Before the present atheistical, pagan or merely indifferent era, Wales was traditionally associated with Nonconformism and the communion and *hwyl* of the chapel but, as elsewhere, the church, Catholic and, later, Anglican, came first, and is even more deeply rooted. The sadly abandoned and decaying St Teilo's church at Llandeilo Tal-y-bont, Pontarddulais, near Swansea, was dismantled numbered stone by stone and transported to St Fagans National Museum of History near Cardiff (Art Fund Museum of the Year 2019), where it has been painstakingly reconstructed in a project extending over two decades. On the basis of evidence revealed under centuries of limewash the interior has been decorated with inscriptions, symbols and wall paintings, among them vivid illustrations of the Passion, God the Father enthroned, St Catherine, the St Christopher narrative, and an imposing post-Reformation Royal Arms, all recreated in their original places using authentic techniques and pigments. It is a glorious example of how a church of the Tudor period (c.1510–30) would have appeared to its congregation. In 2007, Rowan Williams, then Archbishop of Canterbury, described it as a 'stunning addition to the treasure trove of Welsh history contained at St Fagans'. To the museum's many thousands of visitors, St Teilo's is a paint-fresh visual delight, and perhaps a colourful signifier of the power wielded by the Church over the medieval mind.

A few weeks ago we navigated, with care, the narrow, winding lanes of the Vale of Glamorgan to the village of Llancarfan. Iolo Morganwg knew it very well and in all likelihood as child and young man regularly attended its thirteenth century church dedicated to St Cadoc. It is far less frequently visited than St Teilo's, eight miles off, but more wonderful because it still serves a parish and its decorated interior is entirely original. During the re-roofing of the south aisle in 2005–06 it was found necessary to replace some of the wall plates damaged by death-watch beetle. This latter work dislodged some coats of limewash revealing a thin red line, subsequently identified as the frame of a wall painting. With enormous care and skill over twenty layers of limewash were removed to expose a large image of St George in full armour and crested helm mounted on a superb war horse plunging his lance into the jaws of the dragon, while a king and his queen look on from their battlemented castle and a princess seated on a grassy tump, with her dog on a lead beside her, raises her right hand in a gesture of surprise.

Nor was this all. As the work continued further pictures grew from the plaster. In a window embrasure below the castle of the king and queen a Death emerged, shrouded, worm-infested, a toad squatting on the ribs, part skeleton, part rot. The skeletal hand is holding a well-fleshed hand, pulling the sleeved arm attached into view. What cunning the medieval artist had to withhold from us, if only momentarily, sight of the youthful figure on the adjacent wall, who is being thus led by Death to the burial ground, there outside the window. The young man, smartly dressed, a sword at his side, doesn't realise how close he is to 'drooping, dying, death's worst, winding sheets, tombs and worms and tumbling to decay', as Hopkins put it with an almost medieval admonitory relish. Scholars of ecclesiastical history tell us this belongs to the category of images known as 'Death and the Gallant', and further that the Gallant embodies the Seven Deadly Sins – and they, too, are depicted in a large panel on the other side of St George. Each representation of sin – lust, pride, anger, avarice, gluttony and, in this case, a double vision of sloth, physical and spiritual, the latter illustrated as suicidal despair – is accompanied by torturing demons and suspended over a hell-mouth. It is both revelatory and moving. Looking at those images, silently, one can feel strangely close to the distant generations that congregated in that place on quiet summer mornings.

Between Hersch and Weiss

Sound and Image

DAVID HACKBRIDGE JOHNSON

Not sonatas by Mozart, Beethoven and Franck. With encores by Sarasate and W. Kroll. Not a five-minute *world derniere* buried between warhorses. But a twenty-two-movement cycle for violin and piano. Extremes of tempi, technique, perhaps even endurance. And accompanying paintings: depictions of loneliness, asylums, war, prisons, cannibalism, but also a string quartet, a garden concert, a boy in the grounds of a country house. Not your normal violin and piano recital then. Here is a stage set: the two instruments, yes, but also a screen for projecting the images of painter and playwright, Peter Weiss. And a sound world at first tentative, fragmented, but one that ultimately coheres as it progresses, revealing itself as a rich counterpoint to images and expression. This is the work I heard just yesterday (15 November 2018) at St John's Smith Square, a work played with expressive and scarcely believable virtuosity by violinist Peter Sheppard Skærved and pianist Roderick Chadwick.

The composer Michael Hersch wrote his *Zwischen Leben und Tod* as a cycle to the paintings of Wiess, not I think as mere description of images but as a way of exploring the musical realisations of, as Hersch himself puts it, 'color and motion, of proportion'. This suggests a deeper engagement with image than might be the case with a programmatic approach. This isn't to imply that the music is dispassionate, quite the contrary, more that it seeks to plunge to an essence – how sound and image interact, one might almost say on the level of the vibrational spectrum. Yet, thoroughly engaged is sound to picture, viscerally so.

At first the instruments seem to lay out rules for engagement. Placid double stops on the violin, plucked strings on the piano, harsh explosions of discord, stillness, *senza espressivo*-ghosts. A sense in which certain pitches remain locked into specific behaviours. Gestures in search of coherence or brushstrokes of a painter unsure what to paint. As the work progresses it becomes apparent that these gestures return, not bound by the surface structure determined by the twenty-two Wiess pictures, but threaded through – an additional interleaving that runs in and out of what the listener might perceive otherwise as twenty-two discrete entities. This entwinement is a kind of musical double helix. The gestures retain character and even pitch fixity regardless of the context in which each is found.

It becomes clearer throughout the work that 'gesture' is not merely a metaphorical descriptor; there is a tendency for the very nature of sound production to force the musicians into postures distinct to each sound, whether a certain contortion of the violinist as an extreme double stop is essayed, or the twisting of the body of the pianist as strings are plucked or harmonics obtained from inside the piano. I thought of Beckett's extreme directions for the actor in *Not I* – as if posture and expression are fused. This shaping of the bodies of the performers by the material itself is an additional expressive layer and becomes more noticeable with time; in movements like the disturbing *Cannibal Kitchen*, the contortions of the performers seem to parody the lopped limbs and whetted cleavers of Weiss' painting. Short, stabbing, yet somehow futile flicks of *sul ponticello* or snaps of piano strings put bodies into positions suggestive of dismemberment. Sounds are wrenched into garish *crescendo*, several of which cause the violinist to throw his torso down to knee level as if about to self-dislocate at the hips.

What we have here is almost an opera without words; there is the scenery of Wiess and the characters of the performers, but also the fixed motifs running through and appearing like cartouches on an ever changing rock face – not really in the manner of a *leitmotif* technique as in Wagner but rather like a frieze that is glimpsed through the surface plot of the opera. An aloof set of carved figures that only stand for themselves. A mute hierarchy. Although much of the music is disturbing, even shocking (but never in the mere 'shock-value' sense of the word) the overall effect of this huge but ultimately compact odyssey through the world stripped bare by Wiess's images, is one both moving and offering of solace. The little modal chord figures, the open strings that plaintively grate over them, the hints of Bach (Sheppard Skaeved confirmed the presence of Bach's *Eb minor Prelude* as a musical sign – perhaps just one of the Baroque hints I was able to pick up), the wisps of folk song, the lullaby figures – all these are a welcome balm to sooth the sores of an atrocity exhibition. What tenderness amid the haunted landscapes! – the hints of succour in the wasted colours of *In the Courtyard of the Asylum*, or the violin's keening sixths and thirds of *In the Backyard* falling over the piano's intervals like a slowly tipped bowl of apples.

In case the impression given here is of an etiolated display of anaemic shadows, it ought to be pointed out that Hersch knows when to jolt the listener out of the starved reverie; there are two huge boluses of clotted action: *The Machines Attack Mankind* and *The Great World Theatre*. Here the two instruments tumble over each other in a dizzying display of *moto perpetuo* madness – an Hieronymus Bosch world of orgiastic symbolism physically realised in sound and posture. Tonalities racing headlong into ravines. Arpeggiated lunacy. Paganini turned inside out. Alkan clinging to the apocryphal bookcase. A raucous kettle-ing of material whose only escape is collapse into puffs of rosin and clusters of pianistic evaporation.

Despite these scenes of peril, after over ninety minutes between living and dying in Hersch and Wiess's world, a curiously cathartic sense is achieved; a sense of something endured yet survived, a procession of bleak images in sound that somehow resist despair. It is to be hoped that this moving work reaches more listeners. *Zwischen Leben und Tod* is a unique multi-layered creation and if milestones are needed in the violin and piano repertoire, then this surely is one.

On Primo Levi

1919–87

ANTHONY RUDOLF

The centenary year of Primo Levi's birth provides a good excuse to recall *If this Is a Man*, his first book, a fully formed literary masterpiece. In a crucial episode, Levi is teaching Italian to his friend Jean Samuel while on soup detail, glossing quotes from Dante, who knew a thing or two about hell.

Arrested as a partisan, deported as a Jew, Levi spent almost a year in Auschwitz, and survived thanks to his knowledge of German, solidarity with other prisoners, strength of character and luck. Levi returned home by the scenic route, and told the story of that therapeutic nine-month train journey in *The Truce*, first sequel to *If this Is a Man*. Back in Turin, this latter-day self-styled Ancient Mariner would buttonhole strangers and tell them his story. He went on to have a demanding day job as an industrial chemist and manager of a paint factory.

I cannot separate the writer from the witness: the witness was the writer, and that is how we know he was a survivor; it was the same thing. Only later, with his 'invented' books, could one begin perhaps to make the distinction. In his abundant *oeuvre*, there are at least five masterpieces: the most neglected is *The Wrench*, a novel at once about physical work and about storytelling itself. Another indispensable book in what has become known as the literature of the Holocaust is *The Drowned and the Saved*, second sequel to *If This Is a Man.* Here too, his intellect, imagination and feelings are fully engaged.

I was privileged to publish, to meet and become friends with Primo Levi, an exemplary figure who has much to teach us about engagement with the world. He is a great Italian writer, a great Jewish writer, a great European writer. He created a bridge between literature and politics, between art and science. He was an educator for our troubled times, and would have been at the forefront on issues like climate change, had he lived. As a Jew within the tent, he was strongly critical of Israeli policies.

I have a tape recording of a 1961 Radio Three programme, an anthology of Jewish poets, and there is no reference in it to the Holocaust or to Israel. In 1967, thanks to the Six-Day War, everything changed in the discourse about Jewish identity and diaspora attitudes towards Israel, because Israel was perceived as being at risk of destruction. Since then, references to the Holocaust have been endless. People talk about other genocides (Cambodia, Rwanda) and compare them with Auschwitz. Levi always insisted that we use language with care (words like genocide and anti-Semitism), lest we devalue the currency.

Some serious writers reach a wide audience and they do so because, via a literary style embodying felt thought, they are significant explorers of human nature, of human suffering, of human emotion. Levi was such a writer, engaging and personal. People thought of him as a friend and felt his death as a personal loss. Dwelling on Levi's suicide can be a way of avoiding the difficult questions he raised about life and society and responsibility.

Levi wrote to me that *Shoah*, Claude Lanzmann's film, was 'amazing and cruel'. For me, what Lanzmann said of himself just before he died, applies to Primo: 'time has never stopped not passing'.

---

from The Notebooks of Arcangelo Riffis

MARIUS KOCIEJOWSKI

Arcangelo was always on at me about Rabelais, saying that I must read him, which, some months ago, I finally did and not entirely without pleasure, although I could not warm to the book as a whole. I couldn't get on with the endless buffoonery, which I prefer as snacks rather than as a full course. I am torn between a reluctance to admit this and a willingness to say what I feel except that I think I am probably wrong in assessing the book as I do. Some door to it wouldn't open for me. I'd read Mikhail Bakhtin's *Rabelais and his World* and was wholly in sympathy with his ideas on the *carnivalesque*. It is the most engaging work of literary criticism I'd ever read and so it was with something like shock and disappointment, more with myself than with the book, that I was unable to more fully engage with the work that so inspired

Bakhtin during the most terrible years of World War Two, which is when he wrote his great work. And then I got to Chapters 55 and 56 in *The Fourth Book of Pantagruel* which contain some of the most powerfully imagined passages in all literature. It was worth the journey of over eight hundred pages to get there. The ship that carries Pantagruel and Panurge enters the Frozen Sea and it is there, with no land in sight, Pantagruel, studying the horizon, hears the sounds of voices in the air. He calls for everyone to be silent and listen. The crew, hearing nothing at first, gradually begins to hear them as well although are unable to distinguish any of the words. Cowardly Panurge wants to flee. Pantagruel says, 'I have read that a philosopher named Petron was of the opinion that there are several worlds so touching each other as to form an equilateral triangle at the core and centre of which lay, he said, the Manor of Truth, wherein dwell the Words, the Ideas, the exemplars and portraits of all things, past and future. And around them lies the Age.'

And then he adds, 'I also remember that Aristotle maintained that the Words of Homer are fluttering, flying, moving things and consequently animate.' Plato gets in there too. I'm beginning to think *everything does*. *Pantagruel suggests they may have come to a place where the words unfreeze.* It is a deeply complex passage, as finely wrought as one of Cellini's statues. Oh yes, and Orpheus appears too, but let's not complicate things further. Later, Pantagruel casts fistfuls of frozen words (*paroles gelées*) *on the deck, which, as they melt, emit sounds 'in some barbarous tongue' that at first are not understood by the crewmen. It* is only when the pilot recognising one of the noises as the shot from a small cannon that they discover the sounds are 'vocables from battles joined and from horses neighing at the moment of the charge.' They melt into the sounds of an old battle. Scraps of sound gel into sense. Quite honestly, I'm not sure I'll ever get to the bottom of what is contained in those several passages. They are philosophically inexhaustible. I'd say they are poetically inexhaustible as well as if both crew and reader are brought into some region of the divine. Rabelais would seem to suggest that whatever it is we are looking for may be glimpsed but not held onto. Are these not the frozen words with whom I address a ghost at my table and with which it addresses me? I hear the sounds of ancient battle. Thirsty? I reach for the Oracle of the Divine Bottle. [In an attempt to settle the question of marriage, Pantagruel and Panurge go on a sea voyage to consult the Oracle of Bacbuc ('Divine Bottle').]

Why is there always blood on your shorts? I'll spare Arcangelo here the indignity of direct speech. It was enough that he committed to the page what he couldn't put into spoken language although there were, over the years I knew him, mysterious allusions to something terrible in his life, *something unsayable.* Days there were when I suspect the allusions were bigger than the things they alluded to. Those hints he made were so designed, however, that I knew not to attempt to pick the padlocks in his voice. As much we overstepped the mark at times, most of the time we knew precisely where that mark was. We could not have survived any further trespasses upon our already sinking empires. We would have gone under for sure. I'll present this bit of the story in third person singular because I think that's how Arcangelo would have preferred it, the worst elements of his life told at a more or less decent remove. Sometimes I paraphrase. And when needs be, I steal what he writes and I do so with a clear conscience. It's what we do in our trade.

At some point during the summer of 1952, during the first Eisenhower nomination, which will narrow this down to between July 7th and 11th, the young boy was sick in bed, too ill to listen to the radio, too ill to read, and if his was anything like my own childhood illnesses, he inhabited the peculiar space into which sickness lowers a child of twelve, when it would appear that all the air's particles are fully charged and visible. A few minutes before, he'd made an unobserved visit to the bathroom to throw up and was now back in bed, the room tilting to and fro, when suddenly he felt the presence of someone at the door. The boy, desirous of maybe just a moment's affection, looked up to see his father staring at him, his face contorted with hate. With an incredulity that 'cut like hot shrapnel through the miasmal vapours of physical nausea & pain', he heard his father threaten to beat him in the customary manner. It made no sense whatsoever because, after all, what had he who was too ill to move done? Shame filled him nevertheless, the dirty shame that even the mere mention of that punishment always reduced him to. Already he'd suspected its motive, which had only a nominal relation to discipline; its true nature was power, the warped and degrading use of it. The boy understood this perhaps better than his father ever did and yet, decades later, fully grown, he would write of his father that he was no monster, simply a hard-working man, honest as went his world, who just happened to hate and despise his young son.

Something, though, snapped inside him on that late afternoon in July, which would have been about the time Eisenhower chose as his running mate the sudorous senator from California, "You're my boy" Richard Milhous Nixon. Corporal punishment is the failure of authority and it fell into a young boy's nausea 'like foul insects & vermin'. America would soon begin to lose its authority as well. Countries humiliated by her would cease to play her game and so, too, did the boy decide that thenceforth he would no longer cooperate with the punishment previously meted out to him. Along with it would come hatred of Ol' Glory and the American Way. And this was well before the blue devils of puberty descended upon him. The boy had developed quite a smart little enterprise with comic books, the buying and trading of them. Soon he had outlets all over town. A detailed account of the economics involved is given at some length in his, or, rather, the older man's, notebooks, but I have decided to cast over this an editorial eye. After all, it is not the purpose of writing to bore unless boringness serves an epic dimension, in which event it becomes a necessary ingredient. Great writers know *precisely when to bore. Say, simply, those comic books were, in his* words, 'the current coin-of-the-realm in his peer group.' The boy would head off on his Monarch bike, which *bouche d'ombre won* in a contest, when she composed a eulogy in favour of some breakfast cereal, he can't remember which one. Those were the days of prizes. There were prizes to be had everywhere. You could send away as few as three box tops and get a prize.

Almost always this necessitated the consumption of vast amounts of sugar, for the big companies must have noted Keats's words, 'the little sweet doth kill much bitterness', and this in turn fed the fortunes of the dentistry business in a country where it was *de rigueur* to have the shiny white fangs that so often disguised messy lives. Possession of a bike allowed the boy to push yet further the frontiers of his empire. It took him to where a young woman, stark naked, said to him *well, sonny, see something that interests you?* That event was light years away from the rat-infested imagination of one bouche d'ombre, which burrowed into, and fed upon, filth everywhere. One day the boy was about to set off on his bike with a stack of comic books when his father approached him, clearly looking for trouble. *Where did you get these?* he asked. *They're not the sort of comic book you normally buy.* The boy explained they were for purposes of trade. And he went into some of the economic theory that, as author-in-charge, I exclude here. *Take down your pants.* The boy detected hesitation and uneasiness in his father's voice, almost as if the speaker of those words was requesting rather than commanding him to remove his trousers. *Take down your pant*s, I said. The boy said no. *Don't you* *tell me that, don't you tell me 'no', don't you ever refuse to do anything I tell you.* The father continued to bluster on in this manner for a few minutes while his son stared at the ground, absolutely determined to be unfazed by this latest barrage. A miracle happened; nothing happened.

The father continued to beat him, of course, on at least two occasions in front of family and friends, and almost always at the bidding of his wife, but never again did he punish the son in the manner that humiliated him most. The open hand was thereafter replaced by the closed fist.

The power lifting you

From the Journals, July 1989

R.F. LANGLEY

I

On Dunwich beach, B passes me the *Guardian* with an obituary on Philip Brockbank. I did not know that he had died... nor that he had actually founded the York English Department... nor that he had gone on from Jesus to Reading. Nor that he played billiards. Nor, quite, that his loss would be irreparable to his family. I don't recall what I thought had been happening to him since he was in Birmingham at the Shakespeare Institute.

I know he was one of the two best teachers I ever had – eyes bulging, cigarette chugging, intensely caring and very fiercely exciting. At once I wish I had told him so... and decide to go into the sea... thinking that, of all the people I've known, he knew abut Shakespeare, and that is wisdom of the best sort, which would make him thoughtful about the hot summer, the pale khaki and blue sea, the old foam sliding up the concave middle of the new wave, the oddity of looking back to the beach and seeing a wave break from behind, like a shelf you are on, foam appearing from below its edge, you are on a higher level than the bottom of the beach... then the piled flints, the people sitting, the orange cliff with a burst of sandmartin holes at the top, the blue sky with just a smear of almost-dissolved white cloud. The gleaming facets on the water. The power lifting you. The sea Prospero landed from, Caliban's blinking eyes, a close-up, a reptile's, as he sat on the shingle watching the boat come on the next raised shelf of jewellery, to be bounced through the roaring zone of surf, swung onto rattling flint. Pink Miranda in a sunbonnet. Thunderflies at Westhall, on scalp, arms, neck. Here you half lose your body underwater.

I come out to find the sore on my left leg raw again, the scab mostly dissolved but painless. Sea-changed, I doubt. How golden is the rounding now, Brockers? How particular are the things that matter? This bedroom has two wall cupboards now... two bare-wood doors. The old one, nearest the window all, goes up to the ceiling and its floor is raised 1' 6" above the floor level of the room. The new one, going into. ..what was once ... what? ...the little narrow room with the meters in it?... stops short of the picture rail and goes down to the floor, and, inside, is a foot below bedroom level. Both have been neatly carpeted with oatmeal carpet. The new one is slightly shallower than the old.

The white rendered wall round the bulkhead light, near midnight, the casing warm, its glass hot. Webs around it, ciniflo – I've pulled some away. Moths spread, still, patterning the wall. Three small bloodveins... though one has neater pointing to its wings than the other two and seems to lack any of the necessary black dots. A fourth comes. Two common carpets, no doubts here, complex marbles patterns suit the book exactly and there is even the thin dark line up the middle of the outer white line which distinguishes this species. A setaceous Hebrew character, I think... certainly not just a Hebrew character. But there are slight differences; this is a bigger, blundering creature, flicking and flacking and nearly trapped by webs, or running on the torch and banging at that. A fanfoot, but a female without fanned feet... pale dusty gold all over with the spaced lines of gold thread winding and looping across... straight back edge to wings, almost straight black line starting just in from the wing tips. Strange hooked proboscis, hooked upwards. Three nondescript noctoids, one closely-marbled black and grey, one with a black and white spot on the wing, like nothing in the book, the third almost featureless, reddy brown. They settle early and stay still. Five or six common footmen, one dragged under the doorframe head first by a ciniflo... the body being the only sign of the night's concourse left in the morning. Green moth. Micro moth. Plume moth. A small green moth, not quite like a green carpet, though settling like that, while having markings more like a green pug, though not settling like that. A thin-winged white moth, very light, flittering, wings held like a butterfly, just a few scattered black dots... falls... seems dead... from the light. Smaller white, triangular, unidentifiable. A cardinal beetle falls, shrivelling. The spiders stand out on their webs, waiting. We switch off the light and everyone disperses.

At Huntingfield we eat at tables outside the front of the pub, under the sign with the two greyhounds. Children play on a row of bales of straw on the green under the massive tree... two of them little black girls, one in pink, one in bright pattern. A moth flutters from the border plants and, in a second, the heart-and-dart pattern is distinctive.

At Cratfield, Andy looks for spiders and opens the mouth of the Turtle stove. Immediately inside, sitting silently, a full-sized juvenile starling, spotted, staring. He shuts the lid on it, and we open doors, stand back, open it up again. Several times it hops on the lip of the bottom hole – then comes out, flies up to a shelf at bench level, then down to the floor, allowing itself to be herded to the porch, then out, flying off into the trees. It had fallen down the stove-pipe, obviously, all the way from the roof.

The chance of that... within the necessary time. Andy arriving from Kinver and opening the stove while it is immediately sitting within. The opposite of the dead sparrows in the organ-pipes at Gislingham last time. Tao. 'When the wind blows, the sounds from the myriad apertures are each different, and its cessation makes them stop of themselves. Both these things arise from themselves - what other agency could there be exciting them?' (Chuang Chu)

*Poem 'The Stoveplate, for Roger Langley' by Andrew Brewerton sent to R.F. Langley before publication, with the original word 'blackbird' in line 1 corrected by Roger, using Tippex and his own handwriting to 'starling', as in Andy's later published version (*By the North Sea*: Shearsman, 2013); the journal extract, written the morning after the event, puts the fallible memory straight.*

THE STOVEPLATE

for Roger Langley

Her starling eye a long way fallen
In the chimney searches through a fluke
Of slant daylight, a lost lens winking

Late-on in the opened stoveplate
Of an August afternoon. Bird-curious is
The inclination of her neck & yellow

The little moon in her beak: a nice gloss
In the nave at Cratfield. Our two Ruths
Then Eric, look in turn. The stove lid opens

Closes. Soon we'll make a further eye
Of daylight in the south door, & looking out
Askance from eye to eye she'll skip until

The startled space will shiver with departing.
What can one say, that is not given? Who
Address the staved attention of that air?

Why I lifted the cold stoveplate won't recount.
The moon's unnumbered sequence circles
Still. The bird enclosure sequels don't amount.

Our children shout delight in what they will.

edited by Barbara Langley
September 2019

From the Archive

Issue 150, March–April 2003

JOHN ASHBERY

From a contribution of two poems, alongside 'Interesting People of Newfoundland'. Fellow contributors to this issue include Paul Muldoon, Carola Luther, Andrew Motion, Sinéad Morrissey and Jane Yeh.

from MEANINGFUL LOVE

What the bad news was
became apparent too late
for us to do anything good about it.

I walked into a hotel room,
was offered no urgent dreaming.
I didn't need a name or anything.
Everything was taken care of.

In the medium-size city of my awareness
ants are building colossi.
The blue room is over there.

He put out no feelers. [...]

The Fly

PAUL MULDOON

Surrounded as he is by the blood spatter
from the cut and thrust over an idea to which he was but briefly wed,
the fly is washing his hands of the matter

till the smoke clears. A wildcatter
on a rig still lumbering across the North Sea's bed,
surrounded as he is by the blood spatter

and spout of crude, he remembers only a scatter
of crudités, heavy hors d'oeuvres, glasses, remembers seeing red.
The fly is washing his hands of the matter

now a meal in an upper room has once again served to shatter
his illusions. Overcome by the high hum of the dead,
surrounded as he is by the blood spatter

from the cruets of oil and vinegar, the fly is tempted to spray attar
of roses on the aforesaid
'fly washing his hands of the matter',

if only because the internet chatter
points to a city about to cede to the forces of Ethelred,
surrounded as it is. By the blood spatter

you shall know them as you shall know a satyr
by its horse's ears and tail. Instead
of washing his hands of the matter,

the fly might embrace an earth that is irredeemably in tatters
(a banquet of slivers and shreds
surrounded, as it is, by the interplanetary blood spatter),

might heed the pitter-patter
of unborn fly-feet on the stair tread.
But the fly is washing his hands of the matter

even as he contemplates a platter
complete with its severed head, now the centerpiece of the spread.
Surrounded as he is by the blood spatter
the fly is washing his hands of the matter.

Put Off That Mask

Trauma, Persona and Authenticity in Denise Riley's 'A Part Song'

SINÉAD MORRISSEY

This is the text of the 2018 StAnza Lecture

THE OXFORD ENGLISH DICTIONARY definition of lyric runs as follows:

> Of or pertaining to the lyre; adapted to the lyre, meant to be sung; pertaining to or characteristic of song. Now used as the name for short poems (whether or not intended to be sung), usually divided into stanzas or strophes, and directly expressing the poet's own thoughts and sentiments.

It is this latter contention that the lyric, via an authentic and honest 'I'-voice speaker, directly expresses the poet's own thoughts and sentiments which I'd like to investigate further. And I'd like to do so with a double caveat. First, that the subject I've chosen is both so broad and so fundamental to the art of poetry that it is impossible to speak definitely on this subject. Second, that I myself am in a conflicted relationship, not with an 'I'-voice in poetry *per se*, but with an 'I'-voice in poetry which 'directly [expresses my] own thoughts and sentiments', with the notion of what might be termed a transparent 'I'. To be in a conflicted relationship with a transparent 'I' is not to be necessarily – or not always – antagonistic to it. It is to be alert, on the one hand, to the aesthetic and ethical pitfalls of the use of a transparent 'I' in poetry, and, on the other, to be nevertheless aware, indeed at times in awe of, its captivating force.

In her temporary role as editor of *Poetry Ireland Review*, Vona Groarke, as part of her final editorial, answered a set of questions which she herself had set upcoming Irish poets in her previous edition, *The Rising Generation.* One of these questions concerned the use of 'I': 'You're given a choice: either every poem or no poem you write from now on must use the word 'I'. Which do you choose?' Groarke answered: 'Every poem. "I" is probably the most dangerous and dynamic word at a poet's disposal. Introduce it into a poem and the game changes instantly. But I can see why people are wary of it, it's such a sly little thing. Two-faced. Half the time, it's not even interested in itself, it's just throwing shapes.'

So why is 'I' 'probably the most dangerous and dynamic word at a poet's disposal?' I think a couple of obvious things ought to be stated at this point, both of which contradict each other, and both of which are true. In 1993 the Australian poet Les Murray published *Translations from the Natural World,* of which the middle section, 'Presence: Translations from the Natural World', purports to 'translate' the discreet languages of various living organisms – an echidna, a yard horse, a strangler fig – into recognisable human speech. The forms and vocabularies of the individual poems in this sequence appear as bespoke, built from the bottom up to accommodate the unique *thingness* of each subject in question: the snailness of a snail, the pigness of a pig, and so on. Apart from such technical and linguistic bravura, the sequence also, perhaps necessarily, involves a varied and complex deployment of personal pronouns. In Murray's formulation of cow-consciousness, for example, the personal pronoun a cow uses is 'all me':

> All me standing on feed, move the feed inside me.

And when 'me' on its own occurs, it can be any other cow within the herd, as well as the one purportedly speaking the poem:

> One me smells of needing the bull, that heavy urgent me, the back-climber, who leaves me humped, straining, but light and peaceful again, with crystalline moving inside me.
> (Les Murray, 'The Cows on Killing Day')

By contrast, pigs, whom Murray similarly understands as having a plural consciousness, would nevertheless speak in a more abrasive form of personal pronoun, bristling with violence. Hence: "Us all fuckers then. And Big, huh? Tusked / the balls-biting dog and gutsed him wet. / Us shoved down the soft cement of rivers." (Les Murray, 'Pigs'). Throughout the *Translations,* Murray playfully explores the expressive possibilities of mutated forms of the 'I'-voice, and in so doing seemingly erases his own self completely from each 'translated' utterance. Here we appear to be witness to a genuine imaginative engagement with the 'other' at the expense of the human self, the transparent 'I'-voice of the conventional lyric, in poems about animal food, sleep, sex and execution in abattoirs, which expand the possibilities of the poem as an art form.

Or do they? In an interview with the *Paris Review,* Murray stresses the personal, subjective qualities of writing, when he states: 'Readers can take for granted that whoever or whatever a lyric poem is about, it's also about the writer'. He goes on: 'lyric poetry is so thoroughly understood as being subjective that you can use any pronoun you like'. Describing himself as a 'high-performing Asperger', Murray confesses he has always felt more at home in the natural world than in the human: 'I'm not very good at human relations, and it took me a terribly long time to deal easily with people. Even now I use expressions like "the humans". I used that when I was a kid to distinguish between myself and other people.'

No matter how much we may long to escape the tyrannies of an 'I'-inflected consciousness, we can't, because everything we do is expressive of our core nature: our physical demeanour, our clothes, our handwriting, and especially the words that come out of our head and which we place, in our chosen order, on a white page. This appears to be obviously true of a poet such as Sylvia Plath, whose poem 'Elm', reputedly written in the voice of the tree itself, includes the lines: 'I know the bottom... I know it with my great tap root. It is what you fear. I do not fear it. I have been there.' The voice of this poem is clearly at one with the plethora of other agonised 'I'-voice statements in Plath's *Ariel* poems. In a way, a poem like 'Elm' could be described as the opposite of Murray's poem 'Strangler Fig' – not an engagement with an elm tree *per se,* and on its own terms, but an appropriation of the world outside the self for the purposes of a kind of ravenous self-expression. And yet Murray's own explicit connection between his peculiar neurological make-up and his deliberately dehumanised portraits of animals and plants betrays an *equally* self-expressive poetic. And, of course, the translations are just Murray after all. He isn't Dr Doolittle. 'Pigs', 'Goose to Donkey' and 'The Cows on Killing Day' are all elaborate sleights-of-hand Plath doesn't even bother with. Rather than epitomising a humble engagement with what is external to the self, an honouring of the other, you might see the *Translations* instead as an act of gargantuan poetic egotism, in which Murray has the Alpha-male audacity to set himself up as the lone interpreter of the natural world for the benefit of a readership less privileged, perhaps even – given his conversion to Roman Catholicism and his dedication of the *Translations* to 'the Glory of God' – less *ordained,* than himself.

Diametrically opposed to the notion that we cannot help but express ourselves, even when we try not to, is the incontrovertible fact that there's no such thing as a transparent 'I'-voice in poetry to begin with. As Emily Dickinson, master of the dynamic 'I' throwing shapes in a poem, puts it in one of her letters: 'When I state myself, as the Representative of the verse, it does not mean – me – but a *supposed person.*' We could pull the rug out further still, as with the Buddhists, and reject the existence of a stable self *itself,* because our personalities are not fixed but in flux, and subject to radical alteration at any moment. Any anyway, the poem is a transmuting force-field all its own. Drop an 'I' into its odd and tightly bounded territory and all sorts of unexpected things happen. Yeats claimed that 'a poet always writes out of his personal life', but that 'he is never the bundle of accident and incoherence that sits down to breakfast'. And if a fixed sense of ourselves is a narrative we actively construct, day by day, how much more so is the 'I'-voice in our poems a constructed and duplicitous thing, expressed through the metaphor for existence which is all of human language, and as inevitably separate from the maker as a mask or a ventriloquist's dummy? It is a dazzling fiction. It makes all kinds of voyeuristic promises. It is a mendacious hook, this 'sly little thing of an I', offering a reward, premised on emotional truth, which it cannot deliver because it isn't, and can never be, a trustworthy conduit.

Such irreconcilable paradoxes concerning the 'I' voice have been inherent in lyric poetry since its inception, but they have become dramatically more apparent in the digital age, in which our dominant modes of interaction with the external world are all, remorselessly and addictively, centred on the self. It is a strange enough desire to wish to capture what we happen to be looking at in a photograph. And even without ourselves in the frame, there is a heady mix of appropriation, subjugation and hubris in the act of photographing what we see, as we turn the external world into something we can carry in our pocket, thereby arresting the flow of time and the inevitability of death. How much stranger is the selfie, in which the eye of the camera is reversed on the photographer, and wherever they happen to be standing reduced to a backdrop? We have literally become our own relentless focus, stranded, like Narcissus, by his pool – here are my shoes today, here is my lunch, here are my immediate and unmediated thoughts on X-subject – as the demarcation lines between public and private disintegrate and the addictive force of encountering our own reflection everywhere we look proves game-changing in every domain.

Nothing is as electric as an 'I' in a poem. Get it right, and you tender an offer to the reader to enter the world of your poem via the connecting door of reader + 'I' identification. 'I's in poems are undoubtedly recreated in our own image every time we read them. We all know what having an 'I' is like. Indeed, as human beings abroad in a frequently hostile and unstable environment, an 'I' is without question our most treasured possession. But being an 'I' can also be a terrifying experience in which we find ourselves isolated, vulnerable, ill-equipped. In the validation we seek and the factions we form, looking for help with our 'I'-ness is something we can't help doing. And in the poems we read as much as in the lives we lead outside our reading experience, we need all the company we can get. Drop an 'I into a poem and everything changes because no other word proffers an equivalent hypercharged invitation to self-identify.

'I have struggled all my life to never / write about the pepper mill' declares the speaker in Frances Leviston's poem, 'To All Intents and Purposes'; and thereby sets an inevitable set of questions rolling through the reader's head. Why have you struggled? Why the pepper mill? How do the pepper mill and this lifelong struggle against it connect? We don't believe for a second that the poet Frances Leviston has struggled all her life to never write about the pepper mill, that as a toddler, say, (this is a poem in a debut collection by a very young poet after all) she engaged with such a struggle, or that every other poem in her collection *Public Dream* is the site of this struggle victorious. Rather this statement's very impossibility, its hyperbolic logic-defying contrariness, is precisely what arrests us. The word 'I' invites us here, not to step in front of a mirror, but to step into another world, one in which the ordinary rules of play are suspended, and this poem does indeed function as a kind of roller-coaster ride through unexpected, lateral associations, from the Industrial Revolution to suicide.

Where is the sincerity in this, however, and does sincerity matter?

Denise Riley's 'A Part Song' is a thirteen-page poem in interlocking sections which won the Forward Prize for Best Single Poem in 2015. 'A Part Song' relates directly to the questions I've been asking so far about intimate revelation in poetry and its value, and I believe negotiates, with enviable skill, between the need to articulate the experience of traumatic personal loss on the one hand, and the impossibility of doing so on the other.

This very impossibility has several dimensions. There is the impossibility of language itself, and especially of lyric language, to console: the Saussurian gap between reality and language is acknowledged and vast, while lyric poetry itself is presented as increasingly redundant ('Dark little Abbott on your rock, / You will have to speak louder than that. / These days the congregation is a long way out', as Robert Minhinnick puts it in his poem 'Shag'). There is furthermore the impossibility of the 'I' voice functioning as an effective correlative of the aggrieved poet, not merely because the 'I' in any poem is always a *supposed person,* but because grief itself obliterates coherent selfhood. 'Ever tried. Ever failed. No matter. Try Again. Fail again. Fail better', urged Samuel Beckett, and 'A Part Song' is so striking because it consistently acknowledges the impossibility of its own ambition – to reanimate the dead. At the same time, and bound up with its urge to expose its own mission as doomed, this poem searingly articulates the experience of grief and stands as a monumental early twenty-first-century elegy. As Stephen Burt puts it: 'Throughout the book the dead-level, understated, broken-hearted and demotic make their peace with the counter-intuitive and nearly abstruse: it is as if Riley had worked all the way through the storm of poststructuralist critique of voice and lyric and so on and discovered them, after the rain, still standing.'

'A Part Song' is an address to Riley's son who died before the publication of *Say Something Back.* There is perhaps no more traumatic experience imaginable than that of a parent losing a child, and a number of contemporary poetry collections attempt to articulate parental grief. *Say Something Back* could be read alongside US poet Mary Jo Bang's 2007 collection, *Elegy,* for example, also an address to a dead son (both Riley's and Bang's sons died as adults), and winner of the National Book Critics' Circle Award in Poetry. Or alongside Rebecca Goss's Forward-Prize shortlisted collection, *Her Birth,* from 2013, also about parental grief though in this case resulting from the forewarned and inevitable death of a daughter in infancy. With such raw emotional material as the basis of 'A Part Song', the stage is pre-set for an intense reader + 'I'-voice identification, premised on – to return to the definition of lyric with which I began – 'the direct expression of the poet's own thoughts and feelings', and a reader seeking help with her 'I'-ness – or, to state it less kindly, indulging in the pleasure of watching another's pain. The achievement of 'A Part Song' inheres in the way it eschews such easy (and questionable) transparent 'I' + reader identification from the outset, while still constituting a heart-breaking lament. 'A Part-Song' convinces us that Riley does indeed 'know the bottom'; that she herself has travelled back from the underworld of grief in order to speak of it. *Say Something Back* in this context is not only an urgent imperative to the dead to speak; it also constitutes the act of managing to say something back out of the maw of self-annihilating bereavement.

A short lyric opens *Say Something Back* and appears just before 'A Part Song' entitled 'Maybe; maybe not'. It echoes First Corinthians: 'When I was a child I spake as a child' in the lines: 'When I was a child I spoke as a

thrush, I / thought as a clod, I understood as a stone, / but when I became a man I put away / plain things for lustrous'. In 'when I became a man' Riley deploys an obviously non self-referential personal pronoun from the collection's very outset and alerts us to the possibility that the dualism of this poem's title will open multiple interpretative possibilities in what follows: maybe this is me speaking; maybe it's not; maybe the power of lyric can make the dead speak back, maybe it can't. First Corinthians proffers the possibility of transparent communication in the sanctified light of being one-with-Christ: 'For now we see through a glass, darkly; but then face to face' and Riley deliberately subverts this promise with imagery of mud and obfuscation: 'yet to this day / squat under hooves for kindness where / fetlocks stream with mud – shall I never / get it clear, down in the soily waters.' The world we are about to enter in the poem that follows is prefigured here as riven with irreconcilable opposites – as one in which the relationship between author, speaker, and reader is both mutable and unclear.

In keeping with the complexity prefigured here, the title itself, 'A Part Song', may mean many things – for example 'part' as in 'partly finished', 'ragged', 'bitty' – a one-sided argument, waiting, in vain, for the response it expends so much energy trying to provoke. Technically it may refer to the fact that this is a song in parts (twenty parts to be precise); metaphorically that this is a song about the experience of being shattered into parts. In music, a part song is the term for a song composed for more than three voices. Towards the end of 'A Part Song', in the penultimate section, Riley confesses, echoing Eliot's original title for 'The Waste Land', *he do the police in different voices:* 'She do the bereaved in different voices / For the point of this address is to prod / And shepherd you back within range / Of my strained ears'.

So who are the different voices of 'A Part Song' and why does Riley use so many? Riley, in places, is undoubtedly present, and in transparent 'I'-voice mode, as in: 'I so want to join you.' The son's voice is mostly in the poem as an excruciating absence yet appears at the poem's end, finally saying something back, though what he says is hardly consolatory: 'My bone dust is faint choral / Under the fretful wave'. There is a speaker, watching and describing the aggrieved mother, who is depicted, often monstrously, in third-person: 'Here's a denatured thing, whose one eye rummages / Into the mound, her other eye swivelled straight up'. And there are other voices too, in quotation marks, who operate as a concerned but dim-witted chorus: 'By now, she must have got over it.' There are also multiple addressees: the dead son of course, yet more surprisingly, the poem opens with an admonishment of the lyric itself, berated for its in-built redundancy in the face of grief: 'You principle of song, what are you *for* now / Perking up under any spasmodic light / To trot out your shadowed warblings?' An 'ardent bee' is the addressee in part xi, and behind all of these addressees are all of the poem's subsequent readers.

In T.S. Eliot's lecture 'The Three Voices of Poetry' he states that poems addressed to one person are nevertheless always meant to be overheard by other people – that the lyric is innately capacious in terms of who can enter it. William Waters in his book *Poetry's Touch: On Lyric Address* makes a different point: 'it is in these cases where the addressee – grievously – cannot hear, that the act of address becomes most convincingly singular'. A dead beloved is the most obvious example of an addressee who 'grievously cannot hear', and there are moments of direct address throughout 'A Part Song' which appear to be unmediated either by additional speakers or by additional listeners, as in part xiv: 'Dun blur of this evening's lurch to / Eventual navy night. Yet another / Night, day, night, over and over. / I so want to join you.' Or in x: 'Even ten seconds' worth of a sighting / Of you would help me get through / This better. With a camera running.' Or in viii: 'Here I sit poleaxed, stunned by your vanishing'. And it is indeed the simplicity of such direct statements which is part of their emotive efficacy. This is writing from across the gulf of a bereavement unimaginable to most readers, a clear voice articulating what it's like. But it is also, very self-consciously, Riley re-enacting Orpheus with his Lyre, the origin of the lyric mode itself, returned from his sojourn in the underworld with his transgressive knowledge, and singing of it. 'The only constant is a commitment to the thing that is song,' as Riley herself has asserted.

One of the many lasting rewards of 'A Part Song' inheres in its very lack of a fixed speaker, addressee, register, emotion or form: indeed, the mutability inherent in its dance between sections is part of its point. In terms of lexis it veers wildly between Miltonian high lyric statement – 'A Part Song' is in conversation with the entire elegiac lyric tradition before it, and especially with Milton's 'Lycidas' – 'For the point of this address is to prod / And shepherd you back within range / Of my strained ears' – and a more contemporary demotic: 'Oh my dead son you daft bugger / This is one glum mum.' Though none of its twenty sections is longer than the sonnet's length of fourteen lines, there is no fixed pattern to how long each section is, nor is there any fixed rule about when rhyme is deployed. Because of each section's brevity, like the bee described in section xi, 'blundering / With downy saddlebags stuffed tight / All over the fuchsia's drop earrings', the touchdown within each section is minimal and – so the logic of this particular section goes – ultimately ineffective: 'Blind diligence, / Bee, or idiocy – this banging on and on / Against such shiny crimson unresponse.'

Verbs and sometimes whole phrases are often left out of sentences, so that, within sections and across the poem as a whole, an impression is conveyed of the difficulty inherent in the act of speech itself under such circumstances. The first line of the second stanza of section i begins 'Mince, slight pillar.' – leaving readers to puzzle out to whom such a minimal cryptic statement is addressed and what it might mean. Section ii ends: 'I make this note of dread, I register it. / Neither my note nor my critique of it / Will save us one iota. I know it. And.' Section iii opens by answering a question that hasn't been framed within the poem ('Maybe a retouched photograph or memory, this beaming one with his striped snake-belt and eczema scabs…'). Such use of an amputated language speaks to the poem's subject of a human life cut down in its prime and is a brilliantly inventive formal equivalent of grief. But it also asks its readers to do the active work of completing such sentences for themselves and, more generally, opens wide the dialogic possibilities of the poem so that it becomes, not just a one-sided conversation between a mother and her dead son, or between a frustrated poet and the lyric principle, but a dynamic and shared creative conversation between author and reader, acknowledged as such within the space of the poem itself. 'A Part Song' demands that we pay attention, specifically to its many gaps, silences and omissions, in sentences, within sections, and in the white space between sections, always threatening to swallow up the text it surrounds. By so doing, the poem pays its readers the complement of trust, and endlessly rewards re-reading.

Nevertheless, at the heart of 'A Part Song' is the blunt fact of a grief that never goes away, and a persistent maddening silence on the part of the beloved: 'If my / Exquisite hope can wrench you right back / Here, resigned boy, do let it as I'm waiting.' Riley 'doing the bereaved in different voices' is very different from Murray doing Australia in the different voices of its non-human inhabitants. Riley's doomed attempt to re-conjure her son throughout 'A Part Song' is rendered sartorial in part vi, in which a speaker tries on various outfits in order to most appropriately demonstrate to an exterior public internal devastation. Nothing fits: 'A wardrobe gapes, a mourner tries / Her several styles of howling-guise: // You'd rather not, yet you must go / Briskly around on beaming show / A soft black gown with pearl corsage / won't assuage your smashed ménage.' It is this acknowledged in-built redundancy of the attempt which is so moving, as though all of the superb craftsmanship of 'A Part Song' – the voices, the rhyme schemes, the forms, the metaphors ('[a]rdent bee'), the tight metrical boxes of each section – are Riley throwing everything she can at the blunt fact of her grief in order to overcome it, and still failing. In this respect, the failure of artistry becomes the equivalent of sincere confession – 'Here I sit poleaxed, stunned by your vanishing' – which in turn – not because but in spite of formal prowess – becomes the poem's emotional and emotive bedrock.

Is such direct expression of deepest grief, in fact, what we keep returning to 'A Part Song' for? Is this the same thing as the reader + transparent 'I' voice identification of which I spoke at the beginning of this lecture? Is it via such statements that Riley is most straightforward, honest, undressed even? Are we, as readers, in taking pleasure in such direct expression of deepest grief, at our most disturbingly voyeuristic?

The more I read 'A Part Song', the more I watch it shift radically between the difficult paradoxes it both expresses and generates, and the more apt the title of the preceding poem 'Maybe; maybe not' becomes. For after all of the relentless exposure of both her own artistry and the lyric principle itself as unfit for purpose, ('It's all a resurrection song. / Would it ever be got right / the dead could rush home / Keen to press their chinos') the most unexpected voice of all happens at the poem's end: the dead son speaks, and in italics, which throughout have been used to denote direct speech. The poem's recurring hope is that by singing well, by giving a masterful performance, the dead can be made to *say something back.* Up to section 20, it hasn't worked, but then, miraculously, it suddenly seems to have worked after all:

My sisters and my mother,
Weep dark tears for me
I drift as lightest ashes
Under a southern sea

O let me be, my mother
In no unquiet grave
My bone-dust is faint coral
Under the fretful wave

Nevertheless, this utterance is laden with so many other utterances – it carries echoes of both 'Lycidas' ('he must not float upon his watery bier unwept') and Shakespeare's 'Full fathom Five' from the *Tempest* ('of his bones are coral made') – it cannot be taken at face value. The presence of italics might also alert the reader to the fact that this is merely Riley "trying on" another voice in the face of the son's persistent silence as a final act of despair (or perhaps of acceptance). Because the voice is made up – and therefore not real – the language is not new, but inherited, as Frankenstein's body parts are inherited – that other corpse reanimated, not by the magic of poetry, but by the magic of electricity.

So it's as though, in the end, the point of the poem is to say that lyric is hopeless, except that it isn't, except that it is, except that it isn't, and so on. An infinity mirror, rather than offering transparency ('now face to face') consists of two mirrors positioned opposite each other, thereby creating the illusion of infinite distance. 'A Part Song', as it shifts from foot to foot, resembles an infinity mirror: as a reader I do indeed feel I shall 'never get it clear, down in the soily waters' – there is so much space and so many switches to navigate.

I'd like to finish with a final look at an aspect of the poem which offers a way out of the simplistic honesty/artifice dualism. In a later poem of the collection, 'Listening for lost people', Riley concludes: 'The souls of the dead are the spirit of language: / you hear them alight inside that spoken thought.' As a philosopher, Riley has written extensively about the power inherent in language to express things beyond the capability or even intention of the speaker. In the introduction to her critical study of this phenomenon, *Impersonal Passion, Language as Affect*, she writes:

It's not just a matter of the unspoken 'implications' of what's said, but something stronger: of how language as the voice of its occasion can also inflect its speakers.

Laments, rhetorical questions, exonerations, comedies of verbal inhibition, and clichés [...] – these all exert themselves as ordinary effects which are, though, no mere embellishments or overtones on top of their speaker's intentions: they can even outrun them. Or they can make their speakers sentiments virtually irrelevant.

This idea of being *played by language itself* turns the poet, not into Orpheus, but into the lyre, and in section xii, Riley muses on this very possibility, wondering if 'the noise / Rolling through me' is in fact her being ventriloquised by her dead son:

Outgoing soul, I try to catch
You calling over the distances
Though your voice is echoey,

Maybe tuned out by the noise
Rolling through me – or is it
You orchestrating that now,

Who'd laugh at the thought
Of me being sung in by you
And being kindly dictated to.

If the souls of the dead are the spirit of language, not just for the bereaved but for everyone, it ultimately doesn't matter whether we think we're wearing a mask or not – writing becomes more a case of tuning in, than of original creation. Our task is to fine-wire all of our receivers to get it right.

From the Archive

Issue 150, March–April 2003

ANDREW MOTION

From a contribution of four poems, alongside 'The Patron Saint', 'A Dutch Interior' and 'The Middle of Nowhere'. Fellow contributors to this issue include Paul Muldoon, Carola Luther, Andrew Motion, Sinéad Morrissey and Jane Yeh.

from THE SLATE SHIP

A spacious case
of temperate air
and this child's slate.
Six hundred years

lost from sight
in riverbed sludge,
then raised and perched
on a plastic pad.

In the mangled rig
and wonky mast
I imagine the frown
of the baffled artist. [...]

Bliss

A Draft of Cantos 29 and 30

NED DENNY

29.

Latona's shining children, at that certain time

the zenith hangs them beneath the scales and the ram,
one on each side of the girdling horizon, seem
to tremble in a perfect equilibrium
till the moment passes and they change hemispheres;
for just so long, alight with a smile, Beatrice stares
at the white point which had entirely mastered me.
'I answer without asking,' she then said, 'for I see
what you wish to hear in the star where every
place and age is anchored; in that perpetuity,
outside of the mercy that is time, past all
comprehension and containment, the eternal
Love unfurls itself in a hundred billion loves...

not moved by self-interest, but so those lives
might flash His splendour back to Him when they say *I*.
Before light feet whirred on this sea, He didn't lie
inert but exulted in timeless silentness;
form and matter – both mixed and pure – shot into flawless
existence like three arrows off a three-stringed bow,
and, as crystal or amber or glass accepts the glow
of a golden sunray instantaneously,
the threefold opus of the Lord came to be
with no delay between conception and resplendence.
Order was created for each intelligence,
the spirits that seem the universe's summits

and from which pure act is led. Mere potential sits
in the lowest position, and between them are
the celestial alloys held together
with such a weave as can never be unwoven;
Jerome said that between the angels' creation
and the birth of the cosmos great tracts of ages lay,
but this truth I expound concurs with what they
wrote at the dictation of the Holy Spirit –
something you can verify, if you search for it –
and is even discerned by reason, to an extent,
for it's clearly absurd that the preeminent
dukes should lack the realm in which their completion lies.

That which I have elaborated satisfies
three flames of your desire... the where and the when
and also *how* these loving powers were made. Then,
in less time than you could count to twenty, a part
of the angels convulsed the lowest element;
the rest of them remained here, commencing this art –
this dance you have before you now – with such intent
delight their revolution never ends. That head-
first plunge was caused by the pride of he you saw, dead
fathoms of earth's gravest darkness holding him still;

as much as he was arrogant, these ones were humble
enough to recognise their sheer existence in

the Good whereby all sight has its origin...
and so their vision was exalted through the fire
of illuminating grace, their will as entire
and immutable as that on which they're centred
(and I'd not have you doubt, but rather be assured
that the reception of God's grace is a 'reward'
dependent on how deeply the heart can be entered).
Revolve what I've said within you, and you will find
enough to make a sanctuary of the mind;
yet since it is taught in your universities
that the nature of the angels is such that these
spirits not only know but desire and recall,

I shall speak further so that you may see how all
equivocating readings tend to take truth's place.
These substances, from the moment that His face
filled them with joy – that sweet visage from which nothing
is concealed – have never left off contemplating
the mystery that it is, are always wholly here,
and hence they've no need for some abstract idea
to hide or make amends for a lack of presence.
Down on earth, though, whilst seemingly awake, an intense
dream beguiles the lives of mortal men; to those who
propagate teachings that they know to be untrue
attaches greater shame, love of the apparent

making so-called philosophy's paths divergent...
though even this is a less reprehensible thing
than those who ignore or distort scripture's meaning.
They don't think how much blood it costs to sow the Word
within the world, nor that the soul of it is heard
by a humble innocence; for the sake of show,
they invent ingenious theories that go
the rounds of the preachers while the Gospel is silent –
one claiming, when the sixth hour came, the moon went
back on its track and engendered an eclipse,
disseminating error with his restless lips...
the fact being that light veiled itself, which is why

that blackest of portents flooded half the world's sky –
and thus the sheep return from pasture unaware
the grass they digest is a confection of air.
Christ never said to his first followers to sow
trivia throughout the world, but rather stood them so
securely on the bedrock of a higher truth
that – as they fought to set ablaze the fire of faith –
the news became both shield and lance. These latter days
a priest prefers to get a laugh than call to praise,

though if people could just glimpse the metal bird
nested in his skull's white hood, whispering each word,
they'd grasp the betrayal of their trust. Anthony's

swine grow fat on this, and all who tender monies
with blank faces where Christ's countenance should glow.
But we digress... return your gaze to the narrow
path, the sacred track, that our way may be shortened;
the true quantity of angels is far, far beyond
human talk or thought, although a specific
number's veiled by Daniel's multitude. The magic
of primordial light, informing with its rays,
is received and breathed back in as many different ways
as those brilliances are various; love follows
the depth and the degree of what a creature knows,
and so each flame's unique... a facet or version

of the immaculate and undivided One'.

30.

Six thousand miles away, perhaps, the sixth hour's

grandiloquence is burning, as this world lowers
its vast shadow down to the level of man's gaze...
meanwhile, in the deep abyss above, the sky's
beginning to lighten so this and then that star
no longer reaches its radiance as far
as our bleak floor, the lucent handmaid of the sun
extinguishing night's lanterns one by one by one
until ending with the loveliest of all; likewise,
by degrees, the strict bacchanal that ceaselessly plays
round the iota which possesses victory –
seeming to enclose the mote it is enclosed by –
faded from my sight, and now my seeing nothing

returns me to love and my eyes to my darling.
If the essence of everything I have ever said
of her surpassing beauty was concentrated
in a single note of praise, still it would be
unequal to the wonder I now had before me...
a beauty that transcends human measure, so
beyond our neat categories that surely no
creature – solely the Maker – has the full joy of it.
More than any comic or tragic poet
who found a pass in his gruelling climb to beat him,
I own myself vanquished at this point of my theme;
for, as the sun's force makes mortal vision tremble,

the mere recollection of that ineffable
smile seems to ransack the stronghold of the mind.
From the very first day that her eyes awakened
a slumbering heart, right the way to this vision,
my verse has sustained its quest and its precision;
but here these words' pursuit of her graces shall desist,
bowing to the unspeakable as an artist
must ultimately do, trusting that a mightier
instrument than they will finally express her
and turning to the brutal stone from which I carve
my song. 'We've come forth,' she said, speaking with the verve
and bearing of a empress, 'from the largest

body to the heaven where the rays are purest...
that intellectual light which love then illumines,
the love of the Good in which holy joy then shines,
a joy wholly unlike any other sweetness;
here you'll behold the twin militia of bliss,
one of them with the appearance of what will be
when His justice reigns'. With the immediacy
of a lightning-strike, scattering the imps of sight,
a living radiance flashed around us, a bright
veil whose lucid swathes made me absolutely blind.
'The love that quiets this sphere,' I then heard within my mind,
'always greets in this manner those who visit,

preparing the black wick of man to be lit'.
With these brief words I became aware I was
lifted, as it were, above my little powers,
rekindled with such new vision that no brilliance
could dazzle me again; alchemical refulgence,
light in the form of a mighty river running
between banks adorned with the miracle of spring,
now met my eyes, and now out of those eddies came
a multitude of living sparks, each distinct flame
entering a bloom like rubies circumscribed by gold;
then, as if potent fragrances sent them wild,
they reimmersed themselves in the wondrous turbulence

(as each one dived, a fresh glimmer emerged at once).
'The sublime desire that swells your soul, urging you
to jot and to understand everything you view,
delights me with its heat and its intensity...
and yet that thirst cannot be quenched completely
until you drink this water'. Thus my sun. 'The stream,'
she then added, 'and all the topazes that seem
to appear and disappear, the flowers' laughter,
are only foreshadowings of the hereafter...
not that they lack ripeness in themselves, the defect being
a reflection of the fact that your raw seeing
still falls short of the nameless truth they preface'.

No just-awakened infant ever flung his face,
famished from long sleeping, towards the milk than I
bent down to the wave so as to make each eye
a better mirror for its soul-perfecting flow;
as soon as they'd been rained on, the stream seemed to go
not along the ground but *round* like a watery
wheel; then, like people who are immediately
familiar when they lose the masks that made them strange,
the blooms and sparks rejoice yet more – and, with that change,
both the courts of heaven are manifestly clear.
Splendour of Jehovah, in whose light I heard and saw
the exultant kingdom, grant or rather lend me

vigour to describe it with strong simplicity!
There's a luminescence there whereby the Creator
is apprehensible to every single creature
whose peace consists purely in the vision of Him,
spreading out in a sheer and spherical beam
greater in circumference than the carnal sun...
its entire white semblance balances on one
solitary ray reflected off the summit
of the primum mobile, out of which it
drinks this power and this serene vivacity;

and, as a hillside doubles itself as if to see,
in the still lake at its base, the tremulous green

of its flower-starred slopes, so I was now shown –
rising in the ambient radiance – more than
a thousand tiers of those who've returned to origin.
If the lower levels gather such light, God knows
the expanse of the farthest petals of this rose
(though my sight wasn't lost but somehow could witness
that breadth and immense altitude of happiness,
there being no diminution with distance or
increased clarity with nearness where natural law
is powerless and our Father rules directly).
Like one whose silence is eloquent, she now takes me
into the yellow of the eternally-

dilating rose that ascends degree by degree,
uttering praise's scent to the sun of endless
May. 'See the convent of the white robe's nobleness!
See our city and how much it encompasses,
the occupied thrones, the last few empty places;
that seat whose prominence and whose diadem draw
your gaze is waiting for the true emperor,
who'll sit there before this wedding-feast receives you...
the one who shall be righteous upon earth, who
will try to set an unsteady people on their feet.
Blind greed's bewitched them like a baby that must eat
but whose very fever, the dark antagonist,

turns its face away from its weeping mother's breast'.

Three Poems

JANE YEH

The Pretender

Being a doctor is easy, you just wear a white coat.
Memorise the files, study the wall.
If a bald man with an oxygen tank wants to kill you,
Move to a new town. White walls, locked door.
If you had a talking car, you'd have someone to talk to.
In the diner: your big fingers tapping out Morse code.
Horn-rimmed glasses: history professor.
Another gosh-darn town.

If a lady with a bob wants to kill you,
Fall in love. (Her pleather coat.)
Meet me in the parking garage.
If a Belgian man calls you on the phone,
Tell him your innermost thoughts.
Your face, broad and flat as a surveillance video.
On the right is a picture of your mother: gone.

If the lady with the bob is here again,
Bring her up on the screen. Burgundy lipstick, snake heels.
Your hands turning the dials.
Also, your unknown half-brother wants to kill you.
There's a prize at the bottom of the box.
Your face like a slab of concrete: truck driver.
Puppy smothering you with kisses.

Quantum Leap

Home is a shape I don't remember any more,
Between an ocean and a tree. The newspaper tells me
The date, I just live it. My time isn't mine any more

Than the air a sparrow breathes is the sparrow's –
The scarf I lost when I was six, my wife's face,
The number of stars on the flag in 1804:

All data. If I knew which button to press,
I wouldn't be here. Take me away
From the whirlpool bath of existence – I can't

Predict the birth rate of insects or make a gun
Out of cardboard. My torso is disproportionately
Long. When I look in the mirror, somebody else's

Face looks back at me. What's that about?
Take my six PhDs, my California tan, my ambiguous
Manbag and freeze-dried hair – there aren't enough

Wontons in China to fill the holes in my memory,
Old friend. I think of inventing the pizza
Or stopping the H-bomb. I think about baseball

In summer, the smell of cut grass. Home
Is a set dressed to look like a cornfield –
Sun in the sky, going nowhere fast.

The Equalizer

Mickey grabs the duffel bag, revs up the van.
Dramatic synth music over everything. Stabby chords.

Being chased down an escalator, waving a gun.
Light flashing off a revolving door: jangling notes.

Yuppies in the bistro braying about stocks.
The city grey as a towel. Boxy rectangular cars.

An alley, a coffee shop, a garage, and a bar –
Who loves you? It's hard work saving suckers

From their own dumb lives. Category is: urban
Extravaganza. 1 HOUR in neon. Hot dogs and ammo.

Night falls like a key change on the asymmetric park.
Time to return to your carpeted apartment

For the news at ten and jazz on the piano.
The dark like a blanket, covering everything up.

Poetry and Music

Exile and Return

SARAH ROTHENBERG

Poet Adam Zagajewski joined the pianist Sarah Rothenberg for a program of music and poetry in Houston, as part of DACAMERA's 2017–18 season theme, 'No Place Like Home'. The myriad meanings of home were explored through concerts of chamber music, jazz and contemporary works . In 'Music and Poetry: Exile and Return', Zagajewski's recent poems interwove with Rothenberg's performances of Bach, Schubert and Beethoven.

THE POET ADAM ZAGAJEWSKI has lived much of his life in exile. Shortly after his birth in Lvov, Poland in 1945, the city came under Soviet rule and his family was resettled in the Polish city of Gliwice. As recounted in his lyrical memoir, *Two Cities*, the abrupt uprooting turned his family's gaze to the past, to the home that had been. Home became a memory, a place in the imagination - and memory became identity. Lvov, the absent home, was inherited from the remembering of others, as Adam left as an infant; the child-poet grows up in Gliwice amid the stories of uncles and aunts, parents and grandparents, seemingly endless stories that will later fill the poet's pages – myth or fiction, dream or reality, stories contradicted by competing witnesses as are all family stories, subject to numerous personal variations. The lost city of Lvov and all it represents are forever present in Zagajewski's writings, from the rhapsodic poem, 'To Go to Lvov' to his most recent books of prose, *Slight Exaggeration*, and poetry, *Asymmetry*.

The next exile came about in the disruptive 1980s, when the authoritarian communist government of Poland sought to crush all dissident activity and severely restrict the freedoms of daily life. Looking westward, Adam moved to Paris, the traditional oasis of expatriates, long welcoming to such Poles as Frederic Chopin and the great national poet of the nineteenth century, Adam Mickiewicz. Paris became a new home, offering streets of inspiration, every block rich with cultural memory and the aesthetic pleasures of daily life that the French have so perfected. And yet, the literary world of France was not an open one. French poetry of the present remained foreign, with greater friendships formed with writers of the past – Paul Valery, Guillaume Apollinaire, Paul Claudel, Simone Weil – than any fellow contemporaries. In Paris the streets become a home in which one wanders in solitude, with a book in one's pocket and endless cafés beckoning. The charms are great, yet the risk of falling victim to a fate like that of Thomas Mann's fictional Tonio

Kröger – remaining always on the outside, looking in – are real.

An invitation from the American poet Edward Hirsch came in 1987, offering Zagajewski a position in the creative writing program of the University of Houston – a position which would bring much needed financial security to support the new life in Paris, and also, unexpectedly, open up a world of literary friendships and professional relationships. For four months a year, after saying farewell to his wife at Charles de Gaulle airport, Adam would settle into life in the alien urban sprawl of this Texan city, unlike any of the previous homes known or imagined. Houston became a kind of anti-Paris: no beautiful streets in which to wander aimlessly, instead highways and shopping centres in which an automobile and specific destinations become necessary. But Houston offered something unprecedented: a community of students and colleagues, visiting poets and writers who opened up a bridge to the rest of the United States. The splendor of Paris's spaces was replaced by the interior worlds of classrooms, readings and a public role as poet and teacher.

Arriving at first with a German-English dictionary and a migraine, over the years Adam relaxed into the new language and welcoming culture. He brought Europe with him, with his personal history and knowledge, and shared it generously with students and new acquaintances. When lonely for old friends he had not been able to fit into his suitcase, he found them in the stacks of the Rice University library – here lived Rilke, Keats, Mann, ever accessible. Now Paris was the distant home, once removed. And the writing program at the university, and the library, and all the associated people connected by love of writing and reading became yet another, albeit temporary, home – always lived within the parentheses of a four-month period.

As Adam notes in *Slight Exaggeration*, his four-month periods in Houston repeated 15 times, amounting to the equivalent of five continuous years. Somewhere in the middle of this, I arrived in town as the artistic director of Da Camera, a chamber music and jazz organization, shuttling back and forth between New York and Houston. A New York editor had told me to look up Adam Zagajewski, and one evening Ed Hirsch and his (then) wife Janet brought Adam to my Menil Collection bungalow for dinner. My distinct memory of that first dinner is that Adam spoke just once. But soon we were spending Sunday afternoons together. I discovered Adam's early collections – *Tremor* and *Canvas*, followed by *Mysticism for Beginners* in 1999 – and a deep and important friendship began.

Our dialogue has always been one of poetry and music. Now that I think about it, there is hidden in our exchanges the passion for the 'other', the liberation of escaping one's own world of self-expression for another, in which one is the visitor, unburdened of responsibility. Music has always been central to Adam's writing, from his first published poem, entitled 'Music', of 1967 to the first pages of *Two Cities*, in which his self-identification as 'a homeless person' – one who 'by accident, caprice of fate, [or] his own fault... did not want – or was incapable in his childhood or early youth of forging – close and affectionate bonds with the surroundings in which he grew and matured' – is quickly followed by his discovery, at sixteen, of the music of Mozart, Beethoven and Stravinsky. Here, close bonds take root. ('Music was created for the homeless because, of all the arts, it is least connected with place.') Not being a musician himself, Zagajewski is free to wander in music's mysteries, culling from the works of Schubert, Mahler, Shostakovich, a seed that becomes a poem. Capturing in the listener's experience a sensation that is unique to music, that is free from the connotations of spoken language and exists in its own realm. And yet, also, the poet is free from an analytic knowledge that would come from a more hands-on relation. Adam's sensitivity as a listener opens up unknown worlds to him that he then reflects back to us in words. He recently wrote, 'Music reminds us what love is. If you've forgotten what love is, go listen to music.'

The influence of music finds itself in Adam's writing even when it is not mentioned. There is the quiet music of the poetry itself, evident even in translation. But there is also - and this is harder to describe - the metaphysical space that his poetry occupies. The message inscribed in the words – (remember 'Mysticism for Beginners', an essential Zagajewski poem) – strives for a world beyond words. Words are, perhaps, the means of transportation but not the destination. We are led to the place of feeling, sensation, and wonder that music also occupies. 'I see three elements in music: weakness, power, and pain. / The fourth has no name' ('Self-Portrait').

Early in the 2000s, Adam and his wife Maja decided it was time to return to Poland. The Solidarity movement had led to change, totalitarianism and censorship seemed to have been expelled, and Poland was then proudly taking its place among the free countries of democratic Europe. Packing up their Paris apartment, they set off to restart life in Krakow, where they had met decades earlier at the university. Adam Zagajewski returned to Poland as a celebrated poet, widely viewed as the successor to the remarkable triumvirate of twentieth-century poets Czeslaw Milosz, Wislawa Szymborska and Zbigniew Herbert who had brought Polish poetry to the centre of the world stage. Translation would no longer be a daily necessity.

I write this on the occasion of Adam's return to Houston for our joint recital of readings and piano music. This is, I believe, the fifth or sixth program in which Adam and I have shared the stage. There are various reasons I settled on the three musical works of the program. I wanted to begin with an absolutely joyous welcome to Adam, hence Bach's Italian Concerto. The two lively outer movements in F major frame a pensive middle movement in D minor, whose floridly ornamented melodic line sings aria-like above the constant bass.

If I were to pick one composer out of the lexicon to pair with Adam Zagajewski, it would be Franz Schubert, whose subtle genius composes a surface calm that, over time, reveals unimagined depths. The *Andante sostenuto* of Schubert's last sonata leads us into a space of fragile beauty. In its apparent stillness, the movement is like the contemplation of a fixed object. The gently rocking bass is comforting, stabile. We hear the subtle shifts of harmony against the constant c-sharp in the first eight measures, the accompaniment enfolding within its arc from bass to treble the poignant theme. But in Schubert, the change of just one note, the shift of a half-step, the smallest interval on the keyboard, redefines our world. The Andante focuses our attention, for with just a subtle unexpected change of harmony our inner universe expands. In 'Childhood', a poem that begins with the songful plea, 'Give me back my childhood / republic of loquacious sparrows, / measureless thickets of nettles / and the timid wood owl's nightly sobs...' Zagajewski builds through reminiscence towards a Schubertian modulation in the final stanza, 'Now I'm sure that I'd know / how to be a child, I'd know / how to see the frost-covered trees, / how to live holding still'. We must not let things go by unnoticed: this is the charge of poetry. To notice within ourselves our emotional shifts, our inner lives; to notice, in the world around us, the change of light on a blade of grass, the warm breeze as it out of nowhere caresses us. The daily miracles. To pay attention.

Beethoven's Piano Sonata No. 30 in E major, Op. 109, the first of the composer's final three sonatas composed between 1820–22, is here for multiple reasons. For one, I played Op. 109 in Krakow when Adam invited me to participate in the Poetry Seminars that he and Edward Hirsch led there in the early 2000s. So for Adam and myself it contains a shared memory. But Op. 109 also tells us something about the idea of home.

Experimental in nature, Beethoven's last works explode many of the structures of the classical sonata form, while drawing on earlier forms of the baroque in order to carry out these compositional feats. Op. 109 is lyrical and poetic, and yet also radical. The first movement alternates between a flowing *Vivace* and a turgid, dissonance-filled *Adagio espressivo*, one section interrupting the other as though the conventional first (fast) and second (slow) movements of a sonata had been cut in pieces and then smashed together. The second movement is a manic *Prestissimo*. And the third movement, a theme and variations, is longer than the first two combined, shifting the work's centre of gravity to the end.

The variation movement leads us on a fantastical journey away from the theme – changes in texture, tempo, character so extreme that the original melody seems barely present, and yet it is there in its essence, hanging on by a thread of memory, reappearing, disappearing. Until we arrive at thunderous, extended trills that dissipate gradually, subsiding into a final, poignant statement of the very theme from which we started – sublimely introspective, to be played 'with innermost feeling' ('*innigster Empfindung*'). And yet, although the theme itself is unchanged, we find that we, ourselves, are not the same. The journey changed us, and the place to which we return has altered both through time and our own new perception.

Home means many things, and it is not always a geographical place. For me, Beethoven's 30th sonata, a piece I first played when I was sixteen, is a home, a sacred space I've returned to many times throughout my life. Music and poetry offer us homes that we can live in all our lives, revisit at will, carry within ourselves and take wherever the outer world of circumstance may send us. Our true refuge may be in these magnificent homes of the mind and the spirit, transportable and infinite.

The Owner of the Sea

a retelling of the Inuit tales of Sedna, 'The Woman Who Would Not Marry'

RICHARD PRICE

This sequence retells the life and death of Sedna, the female being who is at the centre of a number of tales in Inuit shamanist traditions. My poems are in debt to The Sea Woman: Sedna in Inuit Shamanism and Art in the Eastern Arctic *(University of Alaska Press), by Frédéric Laugrand and Jarich Oosten, as well as to more general reading. Some of these poems have been published in the artist's book by Ronald King, Sedna & The Fulmar and in Prototype. My thanks to Ron and to Jess Chandler.*

Who remembers the names of the Owner of the Sea?

'She is the Owner of the Sea,
the Woman Who Would Not Marry.
The One Who Did Not Want a Husband.
The Owner of the Sea.
She is the Woman Who Was Always Having Sex,
the Terrifying One.
The Woman Who Was Always Marrying, Always Divorcing.
She is the Owner of the Sea.

She is – Don't name her.
Say simply 'the one down there'.
She is the Owner of the Sea."

Father and daughter

My first words were an order.
I tugged off a mitten with my teeth, let it drop.
I reached up, commanded: 'Hold!
Hold my hand!' He laughed, but shed a glove.
He took my tiny fingers in his fist.
We walked slowly, claiming the ice,
'risking frostbite', he'd brag, 'for love'.

She keeps saying No

'Nobody is good enough.
She halts each handpicked man
with her own upheld hand,
will not be wedded.
At each affront
her father cowers behind his fingers,
but he won't cringe forever –
the name of Shame's hot-headed little brother
is Rage.'

Punch, stroke, caress

Once I'd punched the last slow thaw of a man
my own father had forced on me
I took a dog thank you for a companion.
I borrowed now and then a young husband
to train up in the trick of touch.

Difficult hair

'She is beautiful
but spends too much time alone –
to comb, she says, her difficult hair.
She's far too close to her frisky dog,
she even calls it Husband.'

Famine

'We'll be punished for this.
It's no coincidence our fish, lately,
have been smaller, if any are caught at all.'

Husband and I

Husband and I have our small island.

When provisions are low
he swims back to the mainland,
collects a parcel from my father.

He returns, head up,
gripping the heavy packet in his jaws
to keep it dry.
He waits until he's close to me
then he shakes all the water off himself,
the ruffian, and we both laugh.

Husband and I

Husband lays with me
again and again.

Famine

'We are being punished for this.

When was the last time anyone saw a fish
longer than a spear-head?

Giant

Already I am a giant.

There must be whole nations
growing in my womb.

Pups

Eight pups: each is dog and each is human,
or they are the beginning of something new.

Pups

Eight sets of pups soon need more than breast milk.
Husband makes daily trips to my father, requesting meat.

        A fatherly visit

        'Why the need for so much meat?
        Doesn't she know food is scarce?

        Is she ill? Has she a real man, now,
        as well as that self-satisfied dog!
        I thought I would make a fatherly visit.

        As I landed on the island
        she was in the distance.

        Before I was out of the kayak
        a pack of young dogs ran up to me

        wagging their tails and yelping, "Grandad!"'

        'Slut'

        'Slut isn't the half of what they call her,
        my own daughter, and she deserves all the names.'

        Birthday present

        'Almost a year passes and perhaps they think
        I have forgotten the outrage, the disgrace.

        When the dog comes to me for provisions
        I place a large wrapped rock in the packet.
        I tie it to his back, explaining it's precious,
        a birthday present for them all.'

Strong current

There is a strong current
between here and your father's,
Husband had told me.
I believe his death was that and simply age,
oh and the burden of so many repeated journeys.

On the day before his children's birthday
he died providing for his family.

I saw him, struggling, as if weighed down
yet not even a parcel in his jaws,

and then I saw nothing at all.

Taunt

My father arrives the following day.
It was meant to have been a celebration.
A shame your 'husband' failed to deliver
my little birthday present for all the 'family'.
Then I knew he had killed him.

Not safe for the nations

It is not safe for the nations.
From three pairs of shoes I have fashioned three flotilla.
I am only sorry I cannot send my children
to the safety of the moon.

A straw for each mast

I use a straw for each mast and with a word all the craft are full size.

The oldest set of children I teach to build stone houses
and then set them off.

These are the first true people.

The next set of children I equip with bow and arrow
and then set them off.

These are the people who live in the South, our difficult neighbours.

The third set of children I teach to be expert traders, expert sailors,
and then I set them off.

These are the people of the West, who always look ill.

The last set of children run up to me
crying, there are no more ships!
Please, mother, keep us safe, too!

You will be safe.
You will be unseen.

These are the invisible people.

Return

I return to my father.

Look, he says, as if nothing had happened,
there is a man here, out of the ordinary.

He's already brought gifts of fish
sharing them with everybody.

He is tall and not from anywhere near here –
he has come from over the sea.

He seeks your hand in marriage.

'Hand.' For a second I look at my hands
but I humour my father.

Seduced

The right song disguises any creature.
When he sang he was a man to me,
more than any local boy.

Reaching in

You may not see my face, he says,
not caring to step out of his kayak
but please, touch my hair.

I reach in, beneath his hood.

My fingers touch. His hair
is soft as down.

Crossing the ocean

I was between sleeping and waking,
ocean and cloud. I was flying.

My arms encircled him –
I clasped my fingers together, held fast.

That morning

I woke to the stink of fish breath.
My lover is a bird-spirit, a fulmar:
half albatross, half gull.

Alone

I do not love him,
but I miss him.

He stays out days
to bring the best back for me,
but fish is fish is fish.

Sometimes

Sometimes I sing to myself?

I imagine my father hearing me,
locating sorrow from a song –

finding me, leading me to safety, taking my hand,
and teaching my abductor a lesson or two.

In the distance

Here he is, finally,
my father –
not a day, not a week,
but a year later,
persuading the waves,
please, if you will,

make way for me.

Not lover

[two miscarriages

[make way for me
my lover had said
and I
made way for him

[not lover, captor]

Father, assassin

He scales the cliff easily.

Since he grips his beloved fish-knife
between his teeth
he has the appearance of smiling.

Rage in grief

When they discovered the murdered bird-spirit
it wasn't the storm his friends called down on us
that made escape
                        impossible
it was the song they sing to this day:
rage in grief.

First to break

My father was the first to break,
pleading like a seabird himself,
Have the girl! Have the girl!
(Please,
let the waves
equalise us in loss.)

He bundled me,
flailing, choking,
near impossible
to throw over

into the blue.

Grip

I believed I was not made to sink.
I bobbed up, found the kayak, and gripped.

                        The fingers

                        'She won't let go.

                        I hack at the tips of her fingers
                        with the fish-knife her mother gave me.

                        The scraps of flesh drop –
                                      Seals bob up!
                        and still my daughter holds on.

                        She won't let go.

                        I hack down to the knuckles
                        with the fish-knife her mother once gave me.
                        The scraps of flesh drop –
                                      Walruses bob up!
                        and still my daughter holds on.

                        She. will. not. let. go.

                        I hack down to the last joints
                        with that old blunt fish-knife her mother once gave me.
                        The scraps of flesh drop –
                                    Whales bob up!
                        My daughter's hands are just stumps.

                        She sinks.'

Welcoming party

When my father finally reached land he was emaciated
but the dogs who found him still found a little meat.

Unusually for wild creatures they didn't kill him straightaway.
They seemed almost human.

They started with his balls and then his prick
and then gave tender loving care

to his fingers: biting, cracking, then chewing them, one by one.

You will have to visit me

You will have to visit me
if you want plenty.

In my new home underwater
my hair tangles easily

and these likenesses
of seal and walrus and whale

are not clasps or hair clips,
they are spirits, caught up in the snags.

I have no fingers to clear them.

You will have to visit me
if you want plenty.

Send me
a hunter, a powerful singer

who will jab me, make me bleed,
but comb my hair softly,

who will release all the animals

with the gentle strength of song.

'The Poet at Work' © Michael Augustin

Animal Spirits: 2

IAIN BAMFORTH

A FEATHERWEIGHT

Truth is light, feather-light even. We have this from the ancient Egyptians who believed that in the afterlife the heart would be weighed on the scales of justice by the god Anubis against the feather of Ma'at, or truth. If it proved to be as weightless as the traditional ostrich-feather, scribes would record the result and the person under judgement would be allowed to pass on the long and perilous way towards Osiris and immortality. Should the heart's deeds have acquired the notoriety of *heaviness*, the heart was fed to the monster Ammit – part lion, part hippopotamus, part crocodile. Ammit was not worshipped; she was a composite creature embodying the fearsome qualities of the natural world as it appeared to the inhabitants of the Nile Valley. For the heart to be eaten by Ammit was to be condemned to the second death of eternal vagrancy.

JEUNESSE ROMANTIQUE

Sauntering down the long narrow deserted valley of the rue Geoffroy-Saint-Hilaire close to midnight I was compelled to stop and gaze at the sight of a whole row of clochards cocooned for the night on the marble ledge outside a row of modern apartment blocks while, across the road, mastodon hulks gleamed white and spectral through the large windows of the grand gallery of the Muséum d'Histoire naturelle. Marooned in moonshine, these men were sleeping on sheets of corrugated cardboard and old newspapers laid over the heating ducts. Peering out of the windows at them were the skeletal relics of the Cretaceous. And I was Frédéric Moreau in Flaubert's *L'Éducation sentimentale* walking the streets of Paris and discovering their unfamiliarity after dark – 'the great walls of the college looked grimmer than ever, as if the silence had made them longer; all sorts of peaceful sounds could be heard, the fluttering of wings in bird-cages, the whirring of a lathe, a cobbler's hammer; and the old-clothes men, in the middle of the street, looking hopefully but in vain at every window.'

There were no midnight cafés or late-night bars in this part of Paris, close to the Jardin des Plantes; yet for a while I was my younger self, returning home to my pad in the rue de l'Arbre sec from an assignation in a distant arrondissement (rue de l'Arbre sec was just around the corner from the Louvre and St Germain l'Auxerrois in the 1e) and thinking how marvellously all the sounds and sights of Paris lay stranded in pools of nocturnal strangeness. Night is the time when a city reveals itself and people, if you take the trouble to enter into conversation with them, will offer the most remarkable things in exchange for your opening gambit: it is at such times that you feel a city is being lived for what it is and not what it

provides in the way of a livelihood. And Hausmann's marvellous tenements inhabit that other life too until the armies of street cleaners emerge in the first light of dawn – *le crépuscule du matin* – with their noisy hydraulic tools to purge the streets and remove the rubbish. When even a zoologist might care to go to bed, with the sound of horseshoes ringing on the cobbles. The noise of the city has its own rhythms.

All his life Flaubert recommended to his friends Buffon's *Discours sur le style*, perhaps the most rational style-guide ever written, in the knowledge that in his century, the eighteenth, a natural philosopher could for reasons of classicism recommend the scientific attitude as a template and discipline for the imagination. This of course was long before scientific methods had become codified and calcified. Buffon was privy to the thought that staggered the eighteenth century and made time seem like a lake where all the water had evaporated and humans were to be seen trying to keep their balance on its chalky bed: almost all of the Earth's history had taken place before humans came along to write up their discoveries in books and entertain the vertiginous discoveries of palaeontology and geology.

Flaubert worked in the diligent manner of 'sieur Buffon' on time and detail, and brought the important and unimportant together; having read him we notice such things ourselves, and think them novelistic. Even if the only kind of reproduction is on the page, and not between archaic presences in the street leading down to the Gare d'Austerlitz. Henry Céard surprised Flaubert once by telling him how much he admired his novel. Flaubert told him that it was 'a book condemned because it doesn't do enough of that' – and made a pyramid with his hands. 'The public wants books that exalt its illusions whereas *L'Éducation sentimentale...*' – and tilting his hands to reverse his gesture he made it clear that all the hopes he had for it had gone down the chute into a pit of groundless dimensions.

SWINE AND DOGS

In his book about the confluence of ancient and modern philosophical currents in the Weimar era *Critique of Cynical Reason* (1983) Peter Sloterdijk suggests the ancient Greek philosophy of *kunismos* – a major influence on early Christianity – became separated from its historical sources and developed into a type of consciousness that is encountered again and again in history. The rebellious, unkempt, half-naked figure of Diogenes (*kynicism*) gave way to the theoretical knowingness, sophistry and social station of Dostoevski's Grand Inquisitor. This is *cynicism*. Cynicism is 'enlightened false consciousness' – a mindset that understands the nature of Enlightenment but cannot, for all sorts of self-implicating reasons, put it into practice. Cynics are well-off and miserable at the same time. In zooscopic terms, cynics are swine and kynics are dogs, just as they were in Greek times.

That was the attitude of Léon Bloy who, having vented his bile against the English and other significant swine of the day in his tract *Léon Bloy devant les Cochons*, begged forgiveness of actual pigs with trotters.

OUT OF THEIR HEADS

Cordyceps is a genus of several hundred species of parasitoidal ascomycetic fungi which rely (a mild term in the context) on insects for distribution of their spores.

When the *Ophiocordyceps unilateralis* fungus invades the body of a host, commonly carpenter ants, by penetrating the spiracles, its filaments begin to consume non-vital soft tissues. It will then influence the behaviour of the infected ant by means not yet fully understood. Already evicted from the colony by healthy members, the disorientated or 'zombie' ant climbs to the apex of the nearest plant or tree shoot and clamps its mandibles around a leaf vein at a precise distance above the ground (25 cm) with considerable force. This lockjaw is known as the 'death grip'. The fungus then kills the ant, and its hyphae continue to develop within the exoskeleton. Mycelia surge from the mummified ant like tent ropes, guying it even more firmly to the leaf and protecting the carcase from scavenger attacks. A few days later a fruiting body or stroma stalk sprouts from the back of the dead insect's head and bursts in the air, thus ensuring maximal distribution of hundreds of spores – much as the lotus stalk shoots up from Vishnu's navel in ancient Hindu legends of the creation of the world in order to renew the cosmic cycle of death and rebirth.

In Chinese traditional medicine, an aphrodisiac known as yartsa gunbu is derived from 'ghost moth' caterpillars infected by the spores of a related fungus (*Ophiocordyceps sinensis*) found only at altitudes over 4,000 metres in the Tibetan Himalayas: the retail value of the more than 50 tonnes harvested every year make a significant contribution to Tibet's gross domestic product. In Western medical pharmacology, cyclosporin, a potent immune modulating drug most commonly used to reduce the risk of organ rejection after transplantation, is isolated from the anamorphic mould form of a *Cordyceps* subgenus (*C. subsessilis*) that colonises scarab beetles in the temperate climates in the same way as its tropical congener modifies the behaviour of carpenter ants in the rainforest.

PLEDGES

Paradise, at least the natural kind pertaining in the highlands of Guyana or in the valleys of Papua New Guinea, has its truly astonishing creatures (along with its thousands of ingenious parasites), some of the larger mammals being so innocent of humans they make no attempt on being disturbed to seek refuge or find a bolthole. In 1815 Coleridge writes: 'If a man could pass thro' Paradise in a dream, & have a flower presented to him as a pledge that his Soul had really been there, & found that flower in his hand when he awoke – Aye? and what then?'

Well, you might want to make sure you haven't run over a pig before you enter the next village, because you won't be able to exit it unless you have a wad of rupiah in your backpocket to distribute to the machete-armed compensation claimants. I have seen hibiscus *trees* in Papua, and it was no dream; but also a dreary palm-oil plantation and the most abject wooden hovels on the same road.

SEX LIFE OF CATHERINE M.

The calcareous shell squatting in the author's palm would appear to have long ago dissociated itself from the supposition of its ever having tenanted a pious tentative juvenile mollusc.

STILL LIFE WITH FRUIT

Perhaps it is the *encapsulation* of fruit in the Garden of Eden that makes it so appropriate for the story of Adam and Eve's being tempted to eat their way to knowledge: the seed has already individuated into a perfected fruit.

The embodied world confronting Adam and Eve has ceased to be sweet immediacy or pure potential; it is already a future whose beginnings are construed in the life cycle of the fruit. In their innocence Adam and Eve had no awareness of the world, or their place in it; and now they themselves have come into appearance. The moment they discover their nakedness – naked not as they are but in each other's eyes – is also the moment they are outside the Garden. Now it is plain that the finite is pregnant with the future, the kernel with its penumbra. Space ripens. And where two human creatures were blind before they bit into the fruit, thereafter it is Nature which is blind.

That is why fruit – any fruit – seems the emblem of constituted time prior to its decay and the eternal repetition of the natural cycle. And the appetite to know survives the moment of its satiation.

THE MUSHROOM LAYER

Geologists have acquainted us with the 'terminal Palaeozoic fungal event': sedimentary remains from the Permian Period suggest that about 250 million years ago, in what is known as the Great Dying or, more prosaically, the 'Permian-Triassic biosphere crisis' (which was probably caused by dramatic changes in the terrestrial atmosphere arising from paroxysmal volcanic eruption of the Siberian Traps flood basalts), there was massive worldwide dieback of biota including the dominant arboreous gymnosperm vegetation. This allowed for the massive overgrowth of saprophytic fungi, a pattern which can be found in the geological record across the world, irrespective of climate zone or environment, whether marine, lacustrine or fluvial. Palaeontologists estimate that it took the planet thirty million years to recover completely from this dislocation of the carbon cycle.

ASPECTS OF BEING

Some of Charles Darwin's other interests: the formation of coral reefs and volcanic islands, the life cycle of barnacles, the role of earthworms in producing vegetable mould, the sex life of orchids, the form and function of carnivorous plants, the expression of emotions in humans and animals, the effects of domestication on plants and animals, polymorphic breeding systems in plants.

He studied the phenomenon of heteromorphism in the common primrose or cowslip (*Primula veris*), which he termed heterostyly. The plant has two flower types, a pin form with an elongated style and short anthers, and a thrum form with a short style and elongated anthers, and a thrum form which has short styles and elongated anthers. In a paper published by the Linnean Society in 1862 which described his extensive field and greenhouse experiments, Darwin showed that although the primrose, like most plants, is a hermaphrodite, the functional effect of these anatomical differences was to make each flower type self-incompatible; it has to cross pollinate with the other form in order to propagate. Sexual differentiation even for hermaphrodites can be an advantage in evolutionary terms.

'I do not think anything in my scientific life has given me so much satisfaction', he wrote, 'as making out the meaning of the structure of heterostyled flowers'.

STREAM AND DRAG

Borges, in one of his stories about imaginary beings, tells of the remora, an actually existing genus of sucking fish (*Echeneidae*) which is well known for its ability to attach itself as a commensual to larger fish and marine species by means of its dorsal fin which has been modified into a suction disc. It has sometimes been called the 'fishing fish' for this very reason, and is still put to use by fishermen in some parts of the world to hunt turtles. According to Pliny the Younger these fish were also capable of battening on to ships and practically bringing them to a halt – and had already altered the course of history by slowing up Antony's ship at the Battle of Actium. (By extension, the remora was to become associated in legal discourse with delays in lawsuits and births.)

In fact, the truth about displacement speeds is more prosaic and yet more marvellous. One of the competitive advantages the British Navy had over against the French, Spanish and Dutch in the long struggle for naval supremacy in the late eighteenth-century was copper. After experiments by Humphry Davy the Navy decided to use it – at great expense – to clad capital ships' hulls, where it acted as an anti-fouling device, releasing toxic copper ions. This prevented the actual 'remora' – clams, mussels and particularly barnacles, not to mention various kinds of worms and weeds – from settling permanently on the underwater parts of the fleet. It is known that an infestation of shellfish on a modern ship can impose enough drag to increase its fuel consumption by almost a half. So Pliny got it almost right with his story of the unsuspected hindrance.

EAT ME!

It is no mere witticism to suggest, as I once did, that cannibalism is the most radical form of hospitality. Here is some empirical evidence:

Paul Ekman, the well-known psychologist and pioneer in the understanding of human emotion, carried out lengthy field-trips in the 1960s to investigate the expression of the emotions among the Fore people, stone-age natives living in the Papua New Guinea jungle who had never previously come in contact with the outside world. He states in an interview about his time there: 'And I was a respected man because they had said that if I died, they would eat me, and they only ate people they respected.'

The natives were alluding to the complete incorporation of others that turns physical bodies into a social body – a congregation. They were describing, with perfect sincerity, the act of endocannibalism, as it is known to anthropologists, in which the body or part of the body of a person from one's own social group is eaten out of love or respect – thereby refuting Marshall Sahlins's contention that 'edibility is inversely related to humanity'.

From which it is but a jump to the health-conscious cannibal: 'But I want to know first *who* I'm going to be eating.'

I HEAR AN ARMY

One of the reasons (there were many others) for Subutai's success as Genghis Khan's primary military strategist – he destroyed first the Poles, then annihilated the Hungarian forces under Béla IV in 1241 and was moving up the Danube to attack the forces of the Holy Roman Empire when recalled east – was the unprecedented rapidity of deployment of his fearsome divisions of Mongol mounted archers.

Each archer had at least one replacement horse (usually several), and since equine blood and flesh were the staples of the Mongolian diet, the horse-herds were not just a means of mobility but also travelling logistics in advance of the supply line. Anything else needed could be scavenged or plundered along the way. Like the ancient Scythians, as described by Herodotus, they carried 'their houses with them and shoot with bows from horseback... How then can they fail to be invincible and inaccessible for others?' These archers fed on their horses, and the horses fed on the churning of their hoofs.

Amdand u khandand u sokhtand u kushtand u burdand u raftand. 'They came and they sapped and they burned and they slew and they bundled up their loot and were gone.' The Persian historian Juvayni mentions that phrase – uttered by a survivor of the Mongol sack of Bokhara – and avows in *The History of the World-Conqueror* that all the horror of the times is expressed in that single quivering line.

'Horses are the survivors of heroes': this sardonic saying therefore has little application to the Mongol cavalry. It could only have come from a later stage of armed combat when the mounted knight had already begun to lose his grip on prestige.

DREAM OF A FISHERMAN

Japanese Erotic Fantasies: Sexual Imagery of the Edo Period (Uhlenbeck et al.), the first modern study of the shunga or Japanese erotic print, ventures three definitions of the ideal vagina: *takobobo*, or octopus, an appreciation of its sucking qualities, *todatebobo*, or trapdoor, a measure of its ability to retain the male member, and *kinchakubobo*, or purse, a measure of praise for its tightness.

There is a kind of laughter 'that has no lungs behind it', according to Franz Kafka. That is precisely the kind of stifled amusement I heard as a student doing the rounds in the medical wards of the Royal Infirmary in Glasgow. Patients with bronchiectasis coughing up buckets of sputum flecked with blood and pus every morning, and somehow still finding reasons to be cheerful.

Katherine Mansfield thought of her lungs as birds, which may explain why so many of her stories are about creatures that seek to fly. She suffered a fatal pulmonary haemorrhage running up the stairs – 'very pale, but radiant' – to show her husband John Middleton Murry how well she was.

ROOMS IN THE ARK

We have to categorise in order not just to understand but to act. That is what the French verb *connaître* expresses (a way of knowing that relies on understanding relations between things and ourselves): its adventitious etymology (*co-naître*: 'to be born along with') could also describe the glistening world re-emerging after Noah had ridden out the Flood.

Children's books grasp the principle effortlessly: the gopher wood Ark is like a floating Dewey system, in which the prototypes of the species are reorganised, male and female, in the barns of cargo-ship confinement, so as to meet the new conditions of God's will. 'Children and animals, two by two…'. It is an archive.

Classification – Aristotle, Linnaeus, Cuvier, Baer – will be everything in the new covenant of being born with knowledge. 'We may therefore say that neither form nor complication of structure distinguishes classes, but simply the mode of execution of a plan.' (Louis Agassiz)

But notice how botany – logically the first science after the Ark had docked on dry land – is shorn of its odorific qualities in order to make it systematic. What counts are the arrangement and number of the flower organs. The ancient theory of primary and secondary qualities was discarded in the eighteenth century, and all the sensory characteristics which pre-Linnean classifiers had included in their identification of plant species – colours and tastes as well as odours – became superfluous. Needless to say the actual uses to which plants were put were of lesser importance too.

(The great French naturalist, Comte de Buffon, who opposed the impersonality of Linnaeus's system and advocated a more idiosyncratic scheme, suggested that animals should be classified on the basis on their importance for humans: this gave prime place to horses, closely followed by dogs, and almost no recognition to insects. 'A fly,' he wrote to Réaumur, 'should not occupy more room in the head of a naturalist than it holds in nature.')

Botany, the master-science, became a kind of geometry. And that may have been because instruments of improved standards made it possible to observe that some ancient qualities were illusory. And so flowers joined the eye in the new optic carpentry.

It isn't dead horses that get flogged but dying ones.

HOW TO SURVIVE IN HELL

The scaly-foot gastropod, *Crysomallon squamiferum*, is a mollusc that was discovered in 2001 at a depth of almost 2,500 metres in the Indian Ocean on a base of mineral-rich hydrothermal vents that were disgorging superheated seawater from deep magmatic chambers. In addition to the extreme pressure and temperature and complete absence of light at these vents, there are also very steep pH, chemical and temperature gradients between the fluids emerging from the vents and the surrounding seawater. These inconveniences notwithstanding, the gastropod prospers. Its foot, uniquely in the animal kingdom, is loricated with scales composed of iron sulphides and other salts. Its shell also incorporates iron sulphide (rather than calcium carbonate) within an organic matrix, rendering it more resistant to predators and better able to dissipate heat. The US military is currently funding research into the properties of its reinforced armour.

It is likely that Franz Kafka would have been intrigued by such creatures. 'All I possess are certain powers that merge into literature at a depth almost inaccessible under normal circumstances.'

A SLOW VIRUS

It's easy to mistake a bite ('Bisse') for a kiss ('Küsse'), as the Amazon queen Penthesilea does after gorging on her dead lover Achilles in Heinrich von Kleist's notorious drama. Only if you're suffering from kuru.

ONEIRIC WHORLS

When you start dreaming of shells, according to Gaston Bachelard, you have finally accepted your solitude, and wish to retire there unobtrusively.

YELLOW

All the conifer microsporangia in the Black Forest must have opened their sacs in the week when I walked with my wife to the Glaswaldsee above the spa town of Bad Peterstal: not only was the air charged with pollen, which could be seen slowly diffusing in the pillars of sunlight between the trees, but our destination had taken on a patina of camboge. All these casually wasted cosmic sperm-clouds sticky as moth-dust had congregated in the space of a few days on the surface of the lake, a small crater-shaped recess at a level well below our steep descent, there to gather thickly over the leeward shoreline in a massive swirl of what I remembered from my childhood was the powdery substrate of the unpalatable Bird's Packet Custard.

'It is better than a little thing that has mellow real mellow', insisted Gertrude Stein in 'Custard', one of her *Tender Buttons* (1914). 'It is better than lakes whole lakes, it is better than seeding.'

Journal and other poems

ELAINE FEINSTEIN

Journal

1
When the sun comes through the study window
    I cannot read the screen
and sit remembering
    the lyric daze
is for the young at 4am
    with rain in the white lilac.

2
Perhaps I was always waiting for the feverish
    days to be over, to come through into calm,
though being old is not without event:
    it has its own suspense and intensity,
 almost its own weather. And winter frightens me:
 wet slippery leaves underfoot, and early darkness
    on unfamiliar streets.
When the wind gets up, as it did last night,
    I could wish to be a stone or two heavier,
not to be lifted so easily from the pavement
into the road. I'm too slight
to have any purchase here and now
on the only living earth.

3
You might feel the old have the least to lose,
as this planet explodes in a war. Not so:
everything that was comforting me
as I slide towards silence
would be taken away

And as I imagine it, I find, the thought of a planet
without humanity appalls me.

I guess nothing exists until someone responds to it.
The intricate mechanisms of the planet
would be an unread poem:
Shakespeare without English.

4
Actus Tragicus, and the lovely promise:
Heute wirst du mit mir
im Paradies sein.
If only it were true.
But at least the Pope says now there is no Hell,
and surely a long sleep is better than
an eternity of pain.
Martin wasn't sure. You get used to it
but even human torture destroys consciousness after a time.
Arnold said the idea they were damaging you was the worst thing.
I remember during childbirth thinking:
well at least I can make sure this doesn't happen again,
before my first taste of a drug that allows you to cheat,

to float up to the ceiling and look down
at the hurried midwife and doctor bent over your body.

Watching Martin battle with all his grace and beauty,
I want to weep at his courage.
Sometimes, when I hear him play a Brandenberg
I remember the front room in Park Parade
where he and Adam came back after school and relaxed
into the joy of music.
To hear them play together made me happy then.
I would creep down from my study just to listen
to the exuberance, the laughter, the tolerance,
making sense of what might have been a bad day,
though I was an invisible audience.

Heute wirst du mit mir...
There they would be, my lost ones:
my father, David and Tony,
Arnold,
Sidney most recently.
Almost everyone I remember with love.
Impossible to imagine them getting on:
My slow good father,
Arnold still angry.
Who would sort us out?
To whom would I belong?

Nobody believes it any more:
that God is life and the giver of life.
A piece of Him is in us all.

What has led me through my life
comforts me now as common sense insists,
in my ninth decade,
that I approach the end of it all.

My father's last words were:
Is it all ending, Elaine?

I want to leave the people I love
safely this side of the river.

Ageing

Ageing is like winter: skeletal trees,
    cold rain, darkness
on unfamiliar streets

but already the fallen leaves are slippery.
    Snow is forecast, the natural world
will soon be dangerous.

    I shall huddle indoors like Miss Haversham
        over her wedding feast in cobwebs, and
remember all the men I might have married

who never understood their good fortune
        or recognised the fire
behind my dreamy brown eyes

    or asked what I thought of the domestic life
        held out to women then
as their only hope of Heaven

even as Judy Garland's voice rose
    above the applause
while her tears began to fall,
    a choice demonstrably wrong,
since the man she loved
        was walking away from her
for ever, and probably into the gutter.

A Letter to the World

When I was young, I wondered
who would be saved. Is anyone?
A whole generation is dying –
most of my friends are gone.
What use was it, all our striving?

So many stars. And planets.
But do they hold
the living or the dead?

What use are we, after all?
We are all forgotten.

Hold on to that and learn to play.

NOTE: Elaine Feinstein was a leading British poet, novelist, translator and biographer. These were among the last poems she was working on before she died peacefully in London on 23 September 2019.

Death, Fevers and Contemporary Poetry

D.J. Enright as an anthologist

JOHN GREENING

AT ONE TIME, alongside their regular 'state of the art' reassessments, the major publishing houses would produce big popular, themed anthologies, invariably edited by a man, and in most cases by Geoffrey Grigson. They still exist to a certain extent – war poetry, love poetry, nature poetry – but tend to be in aid of some topical concern or emerge from literary micro-breweries such as Candlestick Press (with their *Ten Poems* 'instead of a card' series). Appropriately enough, D.J. Enright's first themed anthology, *The Faber Book of Death* came out the year Grigson died (he was one of the contributors, and also reviewed it) and the pattern was quickly set. Enright was hardly a young man in 1985, but he was well placed to continue the anthology tradition, having worked in publishing since the early 1970s and possessing the necessary magpie instinct. The *Book of Death* was followed by *Ill at Ease: Writers on Ailments, Real and Imagined* (1989), which was reissued the same year

(rather puzzlingly, and in the same gruesome red jacket) under the title *The Faber Book of Fevers and Frets*. The themes brightened a little for *The Oxford Book of Friendship* (1991, with David Rawlinson) and finally came the enormous *Oxford Book of the Supernatural* (1994).

Enright's curatorial gifts had been demonstrated almost forty years earlier when he brought out *Poets of the 1950s: An Anthology of English Verse* (somehow managing to edit it while living in Japan) and confirmed in their full maturity by *The Oxford Book of Contemporary Verse 1945–1980*. Of this landmark there will be more to say, and Michael Schmidt cannot be the only reader to consider it one of the books of poetry which most affected him. But it's worth looking a little more closely at what might have been a minor far-off publishing event in 1955 – that anthology from Kenkyusha Ltd, a Tokyo company (founded in 1907 and still running today) specialising in foreign language publications. It only included eight poets: Kingsley Amis, Robert Conquest, Donald Davie, John Holloway, Elizabeth Jennings, Philip Larkin, John Wain and Enright himself. Some of these were barely known. Enright was one of the few who had even noticed the privately printed *XX Poems* by Philip Larkin (or 'Larkins' as he is called on the dust jacket) when he reviewed him in a Catholic journal, *The Month*, having been tipped off by Charles Madge. Robert Conquest had also offered suggestions for the anthology, which in fact made no difference to the eventual contents. His list of names coincided precisely with Enright's own – except for Thom Gunn, whom Enright would have included (according to Blake Morrison in the OUP festschrift *Life by Other Means*) 'had he known the work'. There was as yet no obvious label to aid an editor in distinguishing these from any other post-Apocalyptic scribblers. There had been a leader in the *Spectator* in which seven of them were mentioned by George Scott, but Enright's anthology and Conquest's *New Lines* the year after were together largely responsible (as Alan Jenkins has pointed out) for defining what came to be called 'the Movement'. *Poets of the 1950s* included not only an introduction, 'Poetry in England Today', but prefatory 'statements' by the poets, some of which are still familiar: 'nobody wants any more poems about philosophers or paintings or novelists or art galleries or mythology or foreign cities' (Amis); 'I believe that every poem must be its own sole freshly created universe, and therefore have no belief in 'tradition' or a common myth-kitty or casual allusions in poems to other poems or poets' (Larkin). A mere eight poets, then, yet the editor managed to define and direct the taste of an era in a way that none of our own age's many-headed anthologies have been able to do. Part of the book's effectiveness – although it's all but impossible to get hold of today,[1] and should be reprinted by someone – lies in the decision to allow space for a fair selection of poems (eight) by each writer, a formula Enright returned to for his Oxford anthology.

But before that, there would be a little more specialised selecting. First came *The Poetry of Living Japan* (1958, with Takamichi Ninomiya), a survey of twentieth-century Japanese verse from Tōson Shimazaki to Michizō Tachihara, published by Grove Press in New York. Enright explains in the introduction that he and Ninomiya 'moved through decreasingly literal drafts to what, but for the congratulatory sound of the word, might be termed 're-creations''. Then seventeen years later – following his third novel, a memoir, several books of essays or criticism, and eight or nine poetry collections – *A Choice of Milton's Verse* came out. Interestingly, this was three years before the gloriously un-Miltonic *Paradise Illustrated*. Somewhere in the middle of all this (before he left academia and entered publishing) he put together *English Critical Texts 16th Century to 20th Century* (1963).

When *The Oxford Book of Contemporary Verse 1945–1980* appeared it didn't catch the public's attention in the manner of Alvarez's *The New Poetry* (which featured ten of Enright's poems) or indeed Motion and Morrison's 'British' successor, which so irritated Seamus Heaney.

Yet it has worn well and was reissued in 1995 – in the wake of Bloodaxe's own version of *The New Poetry* – as *The Oxford Book of Verse 1945–1980*. Dick Davis was unimpressed when he reviewed it in *PNR* 19, calling it 'exhaustingly whimsical' and remarking that 'at times the book reads almost like an equivalent of nineteenth-century nonsense verse; as if Edward Lear had been called upon to edit a volume and come up with an anthology of poems by himself, Lewis Carroll, C.S. Calverley and (to show he could appreciate the higher things) Thomas Hood'. Certainly Enright's choices are sometimes unexpected, revealing a lighter side to 'serious' poets, and letting chronology set the tone from the offset with Stevie Smith (b.1902) and Earl Birney (b.1904), both in playful mood. Compared with, say, the *Faber Book of Modern Verse*, which was about to reach its third incarnation in the 1980s, the new Oxford book might have seemed lightweight. And even Edward Lucie-Smith's much less selective *British Poetry Since 1945* (Penguin, 1970) which vied for the same shelf-space, admitted more of the wilder, darker, experimental and fashionable names – including Alvarez himself. At the end of his exasperated piece, Davis quotes Enright's own poem, 'Poet wondering what he is up to' and adds waspishly: 'For "poet" read "anthologist"'.

In certain quarters, however, the anthology's effect was potent. According to Michael Schmidt, when the first edition arrived for review he took it home and found it 'enormously inspiriting':

> I have always told people that a half dozen key poets on the Carcanet list I first encountered there, but that's not quite true because, looking back at the book itself, some of the key poets I have thanked Dennis for leading me to are missing, in particular Judith Wright. But there is Baxter and Hope and others who may themselves have led me in other directions. It was a refreshing anthology for someone so narrowly reared as I was on the Anglo-Irish, Anglo-American poets... [although] my memory has made the book even more capacious than it was, and more open to women than it was (I also thought Gwen Harwood was in it). I am hugely grateful for the presence there of Patricia Beer whose verse and prose I came to love.

Rather than eight contributors, this time the editor had forty, and they were West Indian, Welsh, Scottish, New Zealand, Indian, Irish, English, Canadian, Australian and American. 'Open to women', true – yet there is Hughes without Plath, Redgrove without Shuttle. One might have hoped for Adcock as well as Baxter, or, yes, Harwood or Wright. One might even have expected Enright to exclude himself. Nevertheless, it still feels like an exciting and inviting volume, both retrospective and premonitory. The Penguin European Poets have been credited with a great deal of influence; but here was an editor claiming that the Commonwealth means 'more to us culturally than Europe'. Enright eschews the fashionable, favours the mature, and reminds us of work we might have missed. The Canadian Earl Birney, the Indian A.K. Ramanujan would have been new to most readers, as would the Australian A.D. Hope and New Zealander James K. Baxter. Then there was a West Indian called Derek Walcott. Nor were Randall Jarrell, Howard Nemerov, Anthony Hecht obvious (or lightweight) choices among Americans – they

---

1 The Charing Cross Road bookseller Henry Pordes is currently offering one for £625.

would be regarded as Formalist outsiders today. Come to that, Elizabeth Bishop wasn't the shoo-in she has become, although the selection might raise eyebrows: 'Seascape', 'Large Bad Picture', 'The Shampoo', 'Arrival at Santos', 'A Summer's Dream', '12 o'clock News', 'Manners'. Lowell was, and is represented, but not by anything 'confessional' according to the editor (yet he includes 'Skunk Hour'). Many of the poets display a gift for narrative, which is something Enright is clearly drawn to (in his own work too), and he has nothing against the lighter verse of Stevie Smith, Gavin Ewart, Charles Causley. While he drew the line at protest poetry, he allowed in those who might be more controversial or politically awkward such as C.H. Sisson or Robert Conquest. He knew the field well enough to be aware of new discoveries like Sisson, but also to realise that the time had come for quietly impressive voices such as Patricia Beer, George Mackay Brown or Derek Mahon who was stealing up and singing in the shadow of MacNeice and Seamus Heaney (Heaney was, of course, included). He even found room for Charles Tomlinson despite that famously hostile review which had accused poets in his 1955 anthology of 'confident lowbrowism' and an 'inadequate sense of civilized values'. Yet there are still surprises in the Oxford book. Norman MacCaig in preference to Iain Crichton Smith. Jon Stallworthy rather than Jon Silkin. And survivors: this is one of Kingsley Amis's last appearances as a poet to be taken seriously.

In his substantial and significant introduction, Enright distinguishes his editorial approach from Larkin's (in his 1973 anthology) who chose to focus on poems rather than poets. Yet he is in much the same stylistic camp, reassuring us at some length that he is not a great fan of 'solemn and methodical deformation of syntax', or of difficulty for its own sake: 'The distinction we need to make is between the difficulty of what is in its nature hard to grasp and the difficulty of what the writer himself has failed to grasp.' He hopes to dispel the notion that British poetry is parochial or overly genteel, but stresses that gentility is not to be confused with civility ('they write most fluently of scars who never felt a wound'). His general remarks seem as apt in 2019 as they were in 1980: that 'there is plenty of boring verse around', that 'a lot of interest is shown in poetry today, compared with the recent and probably the remoter past, but not very much of it is disinterested', and 'We are in a region where one is tempted to say there are no laws. But there are: their presence is only to be inferred from what we can tell is an offence against them'. He notes that academic criticism has turned into 'a virtually autonomous activity', and refers us to Arnold. He suggests that interest in poetry is on a par with 'marbles or yo-yo', and refers us to Shelley.

Even after this considerable operation, his other editorial work proceeded rapidly – a *Collected Poems* of his own in 1981, a selection of his essays on European writers in 1983, and in 1985 three books: an entertaining study in prose of euphemism, a verse autobiography (*Instant Chronicles*) and the first of his popular themed prose-and-verse anthologies. Death was not, one imagines, regarded as an ideal subject by his publishers when he proposed it ('*who would buy it? to whom could it be given?* (the answer since: everyone)' writes his OUP editor Jacqueline Sims

in the 1990 festschrift). His own introduction mentions 'great initial uncertainty' and how friends feared 'the "depressing" nature of the undertaking might prove too much for the compiler's animal spirits'. What makes it succeed is his determination to include what he called 'sincere, human – or all too human – material' by (as David Rawlinson says) 'people who may not be very articulate but who have a right to be heard when they have something to say that is interesting in itself, rather than by virtue of the way they say it'. Rawlinson would collaborate on *The Oxford Book of Friendship* six years later and in an essay on 'the anthologist at work' in *Life by Other Means* he explains why Enright made so effective an anthologist. To begin with, he believed strongly in the 'general reader', but he also approached the task with 'a deeply thought-out procedure'. For the friendship book he specified: no moralising, diversity of sources, no generalisation 'but experiences, incidents, anecdotes, anything that gives the impression of life'. Rawlinson explains that he had a 'manner of excerpting' (but didn't reveal it to his co-editor as it 'would take too long') and understood that the arrangement must appear natural and unforced.

Reading *The Oxford Book of Death* today that is precisely the impression, but at the same time one is left astonished at the breadth of reading that must lie behind it. The combination of verse and prose is perfectly effective, somehow comforting, like having both prickly, musty woollen blankets and cool, fresh cotton sheets, but it's not a book to send you to sleep. Enright the novelist knows how to hold his reader (it's a trick he pulls off with his verse sequences too), and he is never far away, one hand to guide us, the other clutching the editorial scythe. The chapters are each introduced by him, and very shrewdly he opts to transfer all titles to the end of each piece in a small font so that the experience is of an ever-rolling stream. A typical few pages takes us from William Empson's 'Ignorance of Death' through two sentences from Justice Shallow in *Henry IV, ii,*, to an epitaph from a churchyard in Upton-on-Severn, some Homer (tr. Cowper), some La Fontaine (tr. Edward Marsh) and over the page to Blunden's 'The Midnight Skaters'. The absence of a title is arresting and most effective: we are plunged straight in to 'The hop-poles stand in cones...'. This is an approach he maintains in all subsequent anthologies.

The Faber Book of Fevers and Frets (1989) is not on the face of it as promising a field, and Enright's introduction strikes a somewhat defensive note, reminding us of Yeats's belief that passive suffering was 'no theme for poetry', admitting that earlier eras regarded death as the really big subject and felt that 'what led up to it, unless it occurred on a notable battlefield, was of no great consequence'. Nevertheless, the anthology is fascinating and characteristically wide-ranging. It's extraordinary to recall that he must at about the same time have been revising the revised Scott Moncrieff translation of Proust in six volumes, which was reissued to great acclaim in 1992. The work must at least have overlapped with *The Oxford Book of Friendship* (1991). This, the first of his last two anthologies (now with OUP rather than Faber) has dated rather more than the others, although it's not for lack of a broad perspective. The first of its twelve sections alone

(*The Nature of Friendship*) offers us Milton, Plato, Dickinson, Aristotle, Dryden, Cicero, Ecclesiastes, Bacon, Epicurus, Hazlitt, Johnson, Pope, Swift, C.S. Lewis, Randolph Bourne, Proust, Thoreau, Emerson, Santayana, Montaigne, St Augustine, Burton, Browne, Connolly, Lepp, Burke, La Rochefoucauld, Voltaire, Clarence Day, Schopenhauer, Lawrence, Samuel Tuke, Erasmus, Nietzsche, Ogden Nash and Cole Porter. What it doesn't have, inevitably, is any awareness of how the word 'friend' has been remoulded over three decades by Facebook and gender fluidity – and even by certain comedy shows (which Enright the TV critic – see his *Fields of Vision* (1988) – would surely have enjoyed). *The Oxford Book of the Supernatural* (1994) on the other hand holds up well, although its 550 pages are rather heavily weighted in favour of prose, and one ghost story can sound much like another. Editing solo once again, he draws on a wide field of earlier literature (especially Victorian) and appropriate modern texts (unafraid to include Colin Wilson or Michael Bentine) but there is not a great deal of contemporary verse. This might confirm the suspicion that among writers and the general public today there is more of a taboo about the possibility of survival than there is about death itself; but it could also suggest that Enright wasn't at this stage of his life looking far enough among available contemporary poems. Charles Causley's excellent ghost poems should have found a place – and what of Ted Hughes, or James Merrill and his Ouija board? Yet there are beautiful, unexpected juxtapositions such as Rosamond Lehmann's visionary encounter with her late daughter, Sally, followed by the sonnet, 'Sometimes' by P.J. Kavanagh, who had been married to her.

Such collections have a healthy readership when they appear and (assuredly in the case of *Death*) a long shelf life. But in the end it is those that set down a marker for the poetry of a particular age that are important. The 1955 anthology did its work and was then forgotten, like one of those film sets abandoned while the film itself becomes a popular classic. At the very least, without *Poets of the 1950s* British poetry would have looked rather different. And as for what it came to look like compared with the rest of the English-speaking world – there are few more enjoyable ways way to find out than to read D.J. Enright's *Oxford Book of Verse 1945–1980*.

Four Poems

ANGELA LEIGHTON

Swing Song

Winging it up, up, in the brace of a frame,
winging it, high as no-holds, into clear air,
scuffing the trodden turf where once a scare,
a hairy centipede, pedalled on too many feet
into my sandpit, stopped, then dived underneath –
so up, higher, disdaining the baby play
of *oopla! oops-a-daisy!* all that sandfall
raining down from handfuls into small hills,
I kicked against my invaded private ground –
flight, my aim: its rise, swipe, rebound –

till something earthy, bone-deep, snagged and jibbed –
a low-down thud that juddered the swing's clean sweep,
shunting up from a fault somewhere at base
where one steel leg had lifted, enough to nudge
the swinging pendulum, and reach where I
had taken wing above the daisied grass,
the breached pen that once seemed close and safe,
the steady ground that kept its secrets dark.
That jolt shot through my arc of pride and wonder,
riding pitfalls of sand, and what lay under.

Tesserae

my mother and I were alone, leaning from a window which
overlooked the garden... where we were staying at Ostia.
– St Augustine

A sea of stone heaves over tree roots.
Queer fish spill into grass and weed.
Pale square blocks carry waves in quadrants
where a merman sports a swimming tail
though earth has shifted it out of true,
puckered its scales and smudged its line.
Now he's stone-dry, floored forever,
pocked and dulled by centuries of weather.

A flat-fish pans the sun's round disc.
A snagged Medusa treads huge fronds.
Tentacular as handy flares
her knotty feelers twist and tangle –
she keeps a grim petrific stare.
Elsewhere the picture runs aground
in loose chippings, broken bits
of gods and beasts where nothing fits.

Those pines dig in, and turn their heads.
Might ghosts go tip-toe over these stones?
So Neptune drives his posse of dolphins
under and over, where souls used to go
across the waters, beyond what's dreamed –
riding their drowning, homeward somehow.
Now sorrel and vetch unstitch the pieces,
puzzle the point of art's devices.

These cracked wine jars have long run dry.
Marble latrines don't flush their drains.
Was it here he watched his mother die
in a last hotel before the homing sea –
(for Carthage bound, but earthed instead
in Ostia's crowded burial ground),
where dolphins ferry lost souls across a floor –
dream-hardy travellers bound for another shore?

The day is late, the sun going down.
Small tesserae lost in the burying ground
become stone tears, for his grief or mine.
I stoop to fit a wedge-angled chip
into the picture, but make nothing of it.
In the setting sun the pines grow darker.
Such absence presses in the bat-quickened light...
How many gather, lapsed into hindsight.

St Lucy's Day, Sicily

for Gillian Beer

For the sharp clear light of winter, Lucy –
patron of writers, glaziers, and the blind;
for insight tested and foresight tried,
for history's bitter workings-out of strife,

like these rusty spikes, the hardware of war
lodged in the limestone's white knuckle-bones,
Cassibile's armistice, its bombed-out homes,
bunkers derelict among the junipers,

and a forlorn shore of myrtles, dwarf palms,
a lighthouse set to some Athenian fleet
long-defeated, or for Sappho, Plato,
Etna's funny Phrygian cap of snow –

and so, for the dark at the heart of light,
like sad news reaching us here in the sun,
Lucy, grant your lucidity's far sight
for the day, short-lived, and the year's midnight.

A Harrowing

He's got me by the wrist, tight as a clamp,
like a naughty child dragged out of hiding.

No one asked if I wanted this way out.
I was happy enough among the asphodels,

at home in the old place, by a forgetful river,
feeling the solid ground under my feet

with the other, unsaved dreamers, weighing
all the irresolvable troubles of things.

I'd far rather stay, uncalled, ungraced,
in the uncertain shadows, out of the glare

of light, the sky's intolerable vertigo –
conclusive heights I never wanted to climb

where all pain, they say, is repaired, all despair
answered, disasters explained, ever after.

I'd rather linger in these same dim haunts,
lost in surmise and none the wiser

for puzzling the unkind ways of the earth,
close to its roots here, underground.

Perhaps I can slip my wrist from his clutch
and return – to the shades, and fields full of flowers.

Poetic Enigmas

The Penguin Book of the Prose Poem: From Baudelaire to Anne Carson, edited by Jeremy Noel–Tod (Penguin) £25

N.S. THOMPSON

I LOVE THE PROSE POEM. In particular I love its insouciance as a form and, if one may continue the personification, with its complete lack of concern about its literary status. Ultimately, of course, this reflects the insouciance of the authors who first developed it. Although it simply appeared at first, it was consciously developed in creative ways. Or rather, as we shall see, it appeared in one particular form and was then picked up and expanded by others. At its base, it can be seen to be, or resemble, an internal or external monologue, a diary entry, a vignette, a miniature essay, random jottings or notes to self, or even be a short narrative. But one expects more from it than the above forms, something that makes it poetic. And by that I mean it has an ambiguity of meaning that allows it to resonate on several levels. Nevertheless, it is a literary enigma: is it prose masquerading as a poem or a poem masquerading as prose? If it is an enigma, a hybrid or whatever term one wishes to choose, it has proved a highly effective form in which to express and move the emotions and stimulate imaginative responses in its readers. Having said this, given its enigmatic status, it behoves an anthology to give some context and historical background to its development. In this, Jeremy Noel-Tod's *The Penguin Book of the Prose Poem* is disappointing, especially when one would have liked to see an anthology that seeks to educate and inform the reader about the history of the form, which seems to be the only way of introducing and even explaining it.

The prose poem had an almost spontaneous birth in France in the short prose pieces of Aloysius Bertrand writing in the 1830s. They were published posthumously a year after Bertrand's premature death from tuberculosis in 1842 under the title *Gaspard de la Nuit*. But that is only half the title; more fully it is 'Fantaisies de Gaspard de la Nuit' and even 'Fantaisies à la manière de Rembrandt et de Callot'. My edition gives all three on different pages. The last title is the most helpful. We may have no idea who 'Gaspard' is, but we gather that the prose pieces are a medley of scenes drawing inspiration from the paintings of Rembrandt and the engravings of Jacques Callot, as the author tells us in his 'Préface'. Overtly historical, they represent (he tells us) two opposing schools, the philosophical (Rembrandt) and the violently hedonistic (Callot). And the author of this preface is given not as Bertrand but the enigmatic Gaspard de la Nuit. The reader learns this series of forty-nine vignettes, divided into six 'livres', is the work of a mysterious old man who in a park one night in Dijon gives his manuscript to Bertrand to read. When Bertrand goes back to the park to return it, there is no Gaspard. An unknown person says that Gaspard may be the devil, upon which Bertrand's character jocularly wishes the author may roast in his hell.

The work is thus a complex assemblage of personae and styles, with the seventeenth century seen through Romanticism's eyes wearing its 'Gothick' spectacles. It soon lost these trappings in the work of Baudelaire, who was greatly influenced by the work, but created his own mainly visual reflections in a different key. He was the first poet to call for '*modernité*' in poetry (and painting); a call that has to be understood as a reaction against the very late continuation of Neo-Classicism in France and the use of the twelve-syllable alexandrine in poetry. If there is a tendency to see Baudelaire's work as cocking a snook at traditional versification here that has to be tempered with the fact that this particular practitioner was a highly skilled metrist. Indeed, his 'modern' poems are especially well illustrated in a variety of metrical forms in the 'Tableaux Parisiens' section of *Les Fleurs du Mal*. Under the influence of Bertrand's collection, he was nevertheless directly inspired (as he acknowledges) to write his own collection in *Spleen de Paris* (*Petits Poèmes en prose*), again published posthumously in 1869. While he was influenced by the visual arts, as was Bertrand, there is a fundamental tension in Baudelaire between the almost Dickensian sketches of Parisian low life of the poor and deprived and the poet's reaction to what he sees, engendering angst, depression and anger. While not a critical success at the time, the work influenced that other great practitioner Arthur Rimbaud, one of the first poets to link the phantagasmoric and the modern city in many of his two sequences of prose poems *Les Illuminations* (1886) and *Une Saison en Enfer* (*A Season in Hell*, 1873) in the last prose poem of which, he says '*Il faut être absolument moderne*'. If his life was even more chaotically Bohemian than Baudelaire's – at least until his move to Africa, where the chaos was of a different kind – he too was a highly skilled metrical poet, who – in his case – did write damningly of the alexandrine, that bastion of French prosody. It is difficult to say how much these poets were deliberately trying to overturn poetic tradition by the adoption of the prose poem and, one might add, whether they even thought about it in literary critical or theoretical terms. All we have is Baudelaire's desire for more freedom of expression in the prefatory address to his publisher in *Spleen*:

> Who among us has not, in moments of ambition, dreamt of the miracle of a form of poetic prose, musical but without rhythm and rhyme, both supple and staccato enough to adapt itself to the lyrical movements of our souls, the undulating movements of our reveries, and the convulsive movements of our consciences? (trans. Rosemary Lloyd, Oxford World's Classics)

In contrast, the editor of the *Penguin Book* is concerned

to portray the prose poem as indeed a reaction against tradition, a deliberate call to arms against metrical poetry, which is not there in Baudelaire. He writes:

> Without line breaks, the prose poem is free – like this paragraph – to extend across and down the page as far as the printer's margins will allow. And it is in this freedom that we can locate the distinctive feeling to which the prose poem gives form: expansiveness. Unchecked by metre or rhyme, prose poetry flows by soft return from margin to margin, filling the empty field of the page...

Unfortunately, this could also be said of Latin and Old English poetry, the texts of which did not observe line breaks, albeit they could be understood as verse from a knowledge of metre. What is more, this statement implicitly contradicts what the same editor rightly notes in Wordsworth's 'Preface' to the *Lyrical Ballads* (1802) where the poet says there is no essential distinction between the language of poetry and the language of prose. Any difference depends on what the function of that language might be, imaginative expression or scientific explication. This can be taken further, of course: there is no *essential* difference between the language of the prose poem and that of the metrical poem. For example, Rimbaud can exhibit his famous *déréglement de tous les sens* in the metrical '*Le bateau ivre*' ('The Drunken Boat') as much as he can in many instances of *A Season in Hell* or *Les Illuminations*, especially in his depictions of London in the 'Villes' poems. So there is no fundamental linguistic difference here between the metrical poem and the prose poem in these poets, and certainly not in the sense that one is superior to the other precisely because it eschews metre. Again, it is worth repeating that both Baudelaire and Rimbaud, as well as many later prose poets, were highly skilled metrists.

Where there is a difference is in the collage techniques that came in with twentieth century experimentation beginning with the Italian Futurists' *parole in libertà* (words in freedom) and later, in virtually a repetition of this concept, in the 'open field' forms advocated by Charles Olsen in the early 1950s. Here there is true expansiveness beyond known forms and even of known feelings, firstly in the cut up of collage and also in the use of randomness or stream of consciousness (influenced also by the prose of Italo Svevo) that has been a defining feature of a great deal of modern writing. The disjunctiveness of collage is fascinating and appealing, at least to the curious reader, when it takes us into new emotional territory. A great deal depends on where the cuts come, of course. Are they simply to attack normal syntax and critique language usage or to disorder thought processes and lines of imagery to represent new areas, especially associated with the modern world? Perhaps it is better to see collage more as a mirror of the mind's multifaceted responsiveness to stimulation as the term 'simultaneous' suggests, again first used by the Italian avant-garde (*Simultanietà*). Both Eliot's *The Waste Land* and Ezra Pound's *Cantos* exhibit the latter kind, whereas the latest practitioners who would rehearse the snippings of Tristan Tzara and the Futurists seem determined more to create acts of randomness in very often a violent way as, presumably, a protest against order. Interestingly,

Tzara admitted that his famous confession of cutting up words into a hat, tossing them in the air and reassembling them was a fiction. His collages were carefully crafted.

What I hope the above shows is that simple chronology is one way, and a helpful one, to introduce or shape an anthology of the prose poem. It may seem to cut across the plethora of artistic movements, from Parnassians and Decadents on one hand to the Futurists, Dadaists and Surrealists on the other, but the various incarnations of the prose poem do cry out to be seen against some kind of background, almost as if they demand to be read against what else is being written, especially metrically. If the form is an act of rebellion, which is questionable in the nineteenth century, it helps to know what the rebellion is against. When people call for freedom, what does that mean? We have to remind ourselves of the supermarket aisle marked 'Free from' and ask ourselves: free from what? With the prose poem it is not simply a case of 'free from metre' and immediate liberation from its supposed shackles. The implication of a revolution and the heralding of a new dawn is misleading and erroneous. Its origins are more positive than that and beg to be seen as an expansion of expression, a new chamber to poetry's edifice, not a negation of its roots.

These considerations apart, there is also a problem with the anthology's intellectual design and here lies the major disappointment, especially when the editor has included some fascinating and little-known poets and examples (Jessie Dismoor, Fenton Johnson, Anzai Fuye, Lu Xun). The problem is the anthology has no literary apparatus or, to use a fashionable term, a roadmap by which the reader may negotiate the vast range of work: 200 poets mainly from Europe and the Americas, but with some Eastern examples. What of the younger reader keen and curious to know the history of the genre – if we are going to call it that – and to know a little more of the authors and how to judge the contents selected? The editor could have acted more generously as a guide here; indeed, it is only by acting as a guide that some kind of idea of the prose poem can take shape. It is not that this has not been considered, but the solution is unhelpful and the selection gives an extremely skewed version of this hybrid plant. The anthology comes divided into three sections: 'The Prose Poem Now' (2007–2000), 'The Postmodern Prose Poem' (1993–1946), 'The Modern Prose Poem' (1943–1842). As will be seen from the ordering of the dates, the selections run in reverse chronological order and become increasingly sparse in number the further back in time the selection goes. From the 1960s onwards to date there is an almost annual selection with a handful of poets selected for each year (using the date of first publication) and represented by a single poem, comprising 109 pages, whereas the later selections jump from decade to decade with usually only one poet (and one poem) represented in that decade, comprising 177 pages for the 'Postmodern' and 114 pages for the so-called 'Modern'. Therefore, while we have seven poets for 2014, five for 2013 and another seven for 2012, the selection thins radically to one or two poets for earlier years. The designations are also unhelpful in that they confuse purely temporal definitions with more literary critical and philosophical ones, such as the term 'postmodern' itself. Furthermore, how can the last section be 'modern' when it runs from Luis Cernuda's 'Street Cries' (1943) all the way back to Aloysius Bertrand (1842)? How is the reader supposed to understand the grouping of Cernuda's three street scenes of an unidentified town, presumably Spanish, set in spring, summer and autumn, given by an active observer of the period, with Bertrand's evocation of three historical scenes from the Netherlands set in the 1600s or earlier by a fictive persona? How would a reader know the different intentions and personae of the works here? If you are a well-read literary adept, there is no problem, but then why would you need this anthology? It would have been helpful if such an anthology aspired to be evangelical and aimed at both the student and/or what used to be called the general reader. As it is, if you were curious about any selection you would find little help from the book. It includes an index of poets and translators and an index of titles, but they refer simply to the pages of the anthology. If you look under the 'Acknowledgements' you will find nothing beyond the immediate source, which is fine for a poetry collection, but not for the many translations. For example, the last of Bertrand's poems 'Haarlem' (sic) is given as taken from 'Short: An International Anthology, ed. by Alan Zeigler (Persea Books, 2014) and reprinted by permission of the translator's estate (Michel Benedickt)'. Nothing more. If you finally discover the selections come from the collection Gaspard de la Nuit you will find that 'Harlem' is the first in the first section entitled 'Flemish School', followed immediately by 'Le Maçon'; the third selection 'Le Fou' is from the third book 'Night and its Glories'. But here they are given in reverse order of 'The Madman', 'The Mason' and 'Haarlem'. With regard to 'The Madman' the sequence is vital because how else do we know whom the gnome Scarbo might be and what significance he has unless we read the poems that come before?

The other problem with slotting Bertrand last, as if some obscure Frenchman writing quaint historical scenes, is that not only was he very much an influence on poets such as Baudelaire, Rimbaud and Mallarmé, but also on twentieth century poets. A new edition of his work correcting countless errors in the first edition was published in 1925 and influenced prose poems from Blaise Cendrars, Pierre Reverdy, and later – most influentially – the founder of Surrealism, André Breton, who saw Bertrand as a precursor of the movement. In these days of legacy, it can also be noted that Ravel set some of the poems to music, René Magritte named a painting with the title 'Gaspard de la Nuit' and Breton references Bertrand directly in the Surrealist Manifesto.

But how would the reader of this anthology know? In fact, how would they know anything at all? Each selection is introduced by its title and nothing more. If the prose poem encompasses one page then the author is given at the bottom of the page together with any translator. If the poem is longer than two pages, the reader is left wondering who the author may be until turning the third page. And as with the character of Scarbo mentioned in Bertrand's poem, there are no footnotes to any of the works, some of which are highly referential. There is no biographical information on any of the poets, nor information of the original collections from which an individual work has been taken, only the most immediate source in an anthology or in translation. As for the introduction, it is a confusing blend of potted history of the Gallic origins, sketchy at best on Bertrand, mixed with what can only be called 'wall chat' on a whole variety of contemporary writers which even the most inexperienced of readers can see merely repeats in the most simplistic terms what the poems themselves say.

Why Penguin and or the editor elected for this format is not given. Is it that they wanted the anthology to look like a magazine of contemporary poetry? Is this some idea of accessibility? The present reviewer looks at an anthology such as Penguin's French Poetry 1820–1950, edited by William Rees or the Yale Anthology of Twentieth Century French Poetry, edited by Mary Ann Caws, and sees succinct introductions to eras and movements, together with biographies of the individual poets, and representative selections of their work. He then wonders why the reader has been given short shrift. As I have said, there are some extremely interesting historical selections, especially in the 1920s and '40s, but they are almost all single works, and one would have preferred depth to breadth of selected work. There is too great an emphasis on the contemporary, which tends to a sameness of content and intent. One might also ask: what happened to humour? Irony? Both notable in Baudelaire. As to who has been chosen here, it obviously contains the usual suspects, but also a wide range of contemporary poets whose work may be unfamiliar even to hardened poetry readers. I find cataloguing a list of omissions by a reviewer is unhelpful, but the selection could have been lightened by the inclusion of Adrian Henri, say, and Kenneth Patchen, to say nothing of Charles Bukowski. And the fact of only one Italian poet (Montale) is extremely puzzling given the available range of work.

Finally, apart from an inaccurate subtitle, the book's dust jacket prints the full text of Allen Ginsberg's 'A Supermarket in California' as if it were left-justified free verse with arbitrary lines breaks, whereas the original is in ordered paragraphs in fully justified prose format. This contradicts the editor's definition of what he sees as the primary feature of the prose poem, namely that it 'flows by soft return from margin to margin, filling the empty field of the page', i.e. it is fully justified. Perhaps this is a warning to the reader that this kind of anthology is not fully justified. Albeit with some interesting and surprising selections, given the preponderance of work from very recent years, it reads more like a contemporary magazine for a certain in-crowd, which is disappointing given what it could have been by a more judicious selection from a wonderful poetic development.

A Suite of Rhapsodies

Petrus Borel (1809–1859)

TRANSLATED BY JOHN GALLAS AND KURT GÄNZL

John Gallas writes: Petrus Borel was born in Lyons, the twelfth of fourteen children. His early education rendered him atheistic and anti-clerical, solitary, erudite, pedantic and self-dramatizing, with a passion for things Mediaeval. He abandoned his Architectural profession and entered the Romantic Movement, and Le Petit Cénacle, a Parisian, anti-Classicist, revolutionary and Republican band of bizarristes who dressed, spoke, partied, wrote and posed in Freedom. The group included Gautier, Jehan de Seigneur, Devéria, Ourlioff, Bouchardy and Gérard de Nerval. Disappointed by the July Revolution of 1830 ('I do need a *vast* amount of Liberty') Borel and his friends buried themselves for a time in grotesqueries, the macabre, carnivals, Dandyism, and considered outlandish behaviour ('Les Bouzingos').

Petrus Borel published *Rhapsodies,* from which these poems are taken, in 1831. He thought it a book that 'wrote itself', filled with suffering, bitterness, revolution, and what Borel called the 'slag of hot-metal refining'. Enid Starkie, however, the author of the only relatively modern biography of Borel (1954), considers the poems 'mostly gentle and sentimental'. 'There are in *Rhapsodies* however poems which give Borel the right to an individual and permanent place in French poetry.' The book was an intense influence on Baudelaire. Publication created no stir.

Borel went on to write 'gothicky' short stories, the scandalous 'Madame Putiphar' (1838), became a journalist and magazine-writer and, declining in belief and remuneration, went to Algeria as a Civil Servant, where he (according to sources) did, or decidedly did not, do the administration work that was expected of him. He died in Algeria after being removed from his post and digging too long in his garden without a hat. 'Everything God does he does well, and would have left me my hair if He intended to protect me'. There is no known grave.

The sobriquet 'The Lycanthrope', now universally applied to references to Borel, and the subtitle of Starkie's biography, was originally simply Borel's own opinion of his powers and desire to attack conventional society, tyrants, Classicism, traditionalism etc. Borel wrote a short story titled *Champavert le Lycanthrope,* professedly autobiographical, in his collection *Immoral Tales* (1838). The wild seductions, knifings, general bloodshed, sadism, sexual shenanigans, corpses, dissections etc. in these stories have subsumed the nickname into something simply spooky. His portrait, thin, dark-suited, his right hand on the head of a great hound, helps.

These poems were translated by the method used for *The Song Atlas* and *52 Euros* (both *Carcanet*): a native speaker, in this case my brother, translated each word, line, verse and poem into meticulous and practical English: I then 're-poemed' them. I have no beliefs, or even opinions, on the matter of translation, its theory or practise: if a poet gives his/her all to a translation, it will be rather like that poet's own work. It is better that a reader gets my full-throttled versions of Petrus Borel, than a hesitant attempt to copy rhyme, rhythm, structure or contemporary contexts, which will, and cannot help but, lower the percentage of drive.

For the life of Petrus Borel there is really only, in English, 'Petrus Borel: the Lycanthrope' by Enid Starkie (Faber & Faber 1954). The French text of 'Rhapsodies' can be read in Wikisource.

For Jules Vabre, architect

To my dear friend, Jules Vabre:
excellent marrow!
with your little spyglass
on the Fat-Well-Off and their big-bald chins –
you and I must be Martians
on this pale and ordered Earth!
Ah, we must be emmets,
doing what we will, here,
in this pithless Paris,
hither and thither like haywisps on water,
like tonic eddies
through a fly-blown swamp.
Ramblers sans rooves, pewless and
popped from our containers
to live! live slaphappily
like sparrers dancing
on chimneytops!
Wildcats waiting in the wings,
the goggling crowd,
and then, up-curtains please!
we cross
the light-lit stage of Life.

The Olden Captain

*But at last the sailor cries
Land! Land! Look there!*
Béranger

John, my old salt, it must be France! France!
I smell it, like haler breath in our weary sails.
John, am I wrong?
Can you see, there in the fog that hides the harbour wall;
can you see, there aflutter – a dream! No dream!
He's back!

John, John, hug me, kiss me – ah,
mind my old wounds! – caper and trust me
and pipe happy tears.
Can you feel my heart hammer? I'm happy,
I'm happy that God gives His scullion
the sight of Him, fifteen years after all,
my old, exiled King!
He's back!

John, John, how stupid we were to think He was gone.
Somehow I knew in the end He'd come back
with his sword in his hand, from his empty inch,
starved of lordship and awe
to shake us awake with the voice that we knew.
He's back!

John, John, how stupid we were to think He was gone,
who plucked the hand of Rome to His crown,
and climbed to His throne on the ruin of kings,
unbloodied, unbotched,
unhavocked by cutthroats and dogs that eat dogs.
He's back!

John, John, how stupid we were to think He was gone,
who once with one shock-making wave
thunderbolted the world!
How ever could our Shepherd be dead?
Listen! The broken brig drowns in its storm;
and the rocks go down with a crack in their fall,
but He's back!

John, John, we are all for the passing,
but His will clatter the earth,
and there will be wonders, born of a howl,
wonders awful and new,
awful and new as the death of God,
that will rip up the world and the temple-blind.
He's back!

John, John, pull down the pennon, the colours we hate
and nail up this comet-flag
that sweet Heaven has sent us for revenge,
that stuns the eagle in sight of it, sudden to stop,
and the ocean to blow its top in hurrah!
He's back!

John, John, my heart is exploding with happiness -
look at it snapping there, its glory, its blue, its white and its red!
the flying redeemer!
that wraps in its long-house shroud
the palled old corpses, old kings, old Europe.
He's back!

John, John, run to the cannoners, tell them their homeland
has thrown off its yoke, and tell them to thunder
our freedom in shell and in shot!
and twenty times twenty let fly with their battery
to left and to right.
Ah God! this will be patience and patience discharged.
He's back!

John, John, who is that shouting down there on the strand?
a hundred times shouting the same, the same –
is it Him? No, no – 'tis a crowd-cry
angry and only for – freedom!
And... and... there on the top of their banner-jack
is that an eagle? I see the Lord's eagle
clutching at lightning, keeping the storm!

'No, no! It's the old French rooster, Commander' –
and the Captain he heard, and he blanched and back-footed,
and the two old salts, less hearty and fired now,
looked on each other in silent amaze,
crestfallen by nightfall, its reckless elation
like a girl hurling her arms
round the neck of her lover
to find she is kissing the enemy's lips.

Benoni: lament for my brother

His youth, not always kept from need,
touched him with gall, and a wary nerve,
wreckage, sure, of Want's old beggary
broke against Freedom
dunned by a richer mind:
that finished me!

Now he sleeps, my Benoni, and suffers the less,
the first sweet quiet supped for an age.
He has slept one whole day since his eyes milked over
and he pressed my hand in his feebled own
and said, 'You all love me: now let it come!'
He is sleeping, my Benoni.

He is sleeping, my Benoni: come,
tiptoe and see him becalmed; hush, hush,
make no sound to rewake him,
come quietly here in the private Best Room.
Look but speak soft – ah, who would stir him
to suffer the more, his slumber so sweet.
He is sleeping, my Benoni.

He is sleeping, my Benoni! Now, with your unquiet hand,
lift up this curtain and look on his face –
his wide eyes shut, his brow part-paled.
How peaceful, and smiling perhaps... perhaps,
out of a pleasant dream. Listen! A sigh.

He is sleeping, my Benoni, Ah, sad disturber,
you call his name – leave him to absence.
You sob and you shudder, you kiss him
and pluck up the hand that pressed mine.
Do not rewake him... no need for a storm;
in your tempest of tears I too will be shaken.

He is sleeping, your Benoni:
I envy him such fair unfairness.
Poor boy – the mystery of life ungrasped,
his melancholy hour is early done:
the soul, thought-sundering the flesh,
takes to Heaven, ununderstood.
He is sleeping, our Benoni!

A timely corrective

Can't get her out of my heart;
Or find a place for you.
Malherbe

Don't call me cold, don't call me proud,
don't think my heart's a brazen door;
my eye aloof, my smile unkind,
my soul shut tight to soft desire.

You may know much, but not my mind:
think less that I am ice – I too
can love and burn, and promise to be true.

I love with gloomy majesty,
like kingdoms shot with bloody light:
alone, on some old balcony
my lute plucks forth its shimmered scales.

And hid from sight, I count the kisses
lovers share, while in the night
the floating moon rocks with silver light.

The hundred hunters bursting mud,
the brash horns winding in the woods,
the beaters and the howling hounds,
the hue, the cry, the bloody end;

And underneath the setting sun
the hillfolks pipe in glades unseen,
and tread their quiet measures on the green.

I love the fume of frankincense
and manna, and the sweet field-flowers;
to loll, half-nude, at hot midday
on plump divans in dizzy rest:

a pipe, a scented cigarette,
an aromatic tea, refined
to mollify my melancholy mind.

To plunder long-forgotten books
and find new liking in the dust;
unknot some Greek or Latin ode,
try a verse, unearth a gem:

and then the crazy, reeling feast,
the shameless orgy: as I read
my body sinks beneath the weight of greed.

And summer nights through woods and fields
agallop on my pelting bay;
songs of war that wake the steeps,
and fire, and flames! my darksome thrill.

To crush the tin god and his flag;
to splash the blade with blood; to break
the rash invader's heart, for freedom's sake.

Don't call me cold, don't call me proud,
don't think my heart's a brazen door;
my eye aloof, my smile unkind,
my soul shut tight to soft desire.

You may know much, but not my mind:
think less that I am ice – I too
can love and burn, and promise to be true.

to Joseph Bouchardi, Engraver

Thus spake the lion — Phed.

There is something rather ghastly about
Holy Love For Your Country. — Saint-Just

Rest now, old poignard, good and faithful friend.
Rest, cradled in my hand; your country's light
and tired at last. Blood has rivered your blade,
which rings yet from a hundred shocks.

I am well content. We know each other's souls.
You ward my will; and when my killer's arm
thrusts you, throwing a glittered circle through the air,
you hurry forth, and in, to greedy death.

Rest now, old poignard, good and faithful friend.
Rest, cradled in my hand; your country's light
and tired at last. Blood has rivered your blade,
which rings yet from a hundred shocks.

And now you have had your fill. Your prey
has foundered at your feet. The streets are red.
And had your pleasure: to strike a tin god,
screeching twixt his bones, and nail death down.

Rest now, old poignard, good and faithful friend.
Rest, cradled in my hand; your country's light
and tired at last. Blood has rivered your blade,
which rings yet from a hundred shocks.

Such slaughter surely cannot be a crime.
Tread down my childhood, so, when I am a man
I break my chains and stir against the yoke. Beware!
Man counts his days of dirt, and waits his hour.

Rest now, old poignard, good and faithful friend.
Rest, cradled in my hand; your country's light
and tired at last. Blood has rivered your blade,
which rings yet from a hundred shocks.

So – see this cap that rides my shock?
Tis triple-greased with spy-blood.
The scarlet grins at me: tis our banner,
the sainted surcoat of our chosen god.

Rest now, old poignard, good and faithful friend.
Rest, cradled in my hand; your country's light
and tired at last. Blood has rivered your blade,
which rings yet from a hundred shocks.

Tis hung at my thigh; dear penetrator –
still you quiver, ready, and I clinch your steel.
And years to come I'll stud you with gems
like a hero's mettlesome blood-horse.

Rest now, old poignard, good and faithful friend.
Rest, cradled in my hand; your country's light
and tired at last. Blood has rivered your blade,
which rings yet from a hundred shocks.

Whimsy

Birds! Birds! I wish I was one!
The merriest creatures under the sun!

Your sky-easy tacking, your casual care,
Your feathers that fly without Wisdom or God,
Dizzy as cloudlets and fair-weather-shod!
Your trilly fly-hunting that jingles the air!

Birds! Birds! I wish I was one!
The merriest creatures under the sun!

Your games in and out of the gates of the sky!
Your unvarnished voices the Soul understands,
Like echoes of Promised and faraway lands
Where our thoughts and our words are a bitterless sigh!

Birds! Birds! I wish I was one!
The merriest creatures under the sun!

Free of need and jealousy;
Free of ambition and free of pain;
Free of prisons and free of chains;
Free of Bishops and Majesties!

Birds! Birds! I wish I was one!
The merriest creatures under the sun!

No Princes, no Heroes, no Conquering Lords,
No brain-withered Judges with cobwebs for hearts;
No bickering families to tear you apart;
No plotting relations, no ropes and no swords!

Birds! Birds! I wish I was one!
The merriest creatures under the sun!

No flesh-creeping lusts, no voluptuous wrongs;
No slave-making marriage, no Oaths to deny;
Happy in Liberty! Wild as the sky!
Long live your freedom! and long live your songs!

Birds! Birds! I wish I was one!
The merriest creatures under the sun!

True Vine

ANDREW WYNN OWEN

My God, how I these studies prize,
That do thy hidden workings show!
Whose sum is such
No sum so much:
Nay, summed as sand they sumless grow.
I lie to sleep, from sleep I rise,
Yet still in thought with thee I go.
— Mary Sidney Herbert, 'Psalm 139'

'One should never go to God, as it were "on purpose"'
— Leo Tolstoy, 'Thoughts on God' (1900), trans. Vladimir Tchertkoff

1. VINE

The infinite is intricate, a vine
    That wanders and rewinds,
  An inexplicable design,
    One of those marvellous finds
That never disappoint, degenerate,
    Or fail to satisfy the mind's
Demand for narratives commensurate
      With all it must
    Discover and call fate.
      We have this lust
  For clasping what we ought to be,
      Even as dust
Whips up to sweep us under totally.

2. SEARCHING

I pass my days in search of what to praise
    And when I find it there's
  An end of looking, till the ways
    It turns me wire my cares
To stranger outlets, loopholes better suited
    To a lost animal seeking shares
In many-sharded mystery – so confuted,
      Compounded, packed,
    And perilously computed
      That I am wracked
When moving in its blistering ambit,
      Sharply sidetracked
By bliss's restlessness, by bafflement's gambit.

3. LOVE

Elucidate me, tell me what it is,
    Give me an anecdote,
    Some parable. Don't let time whizz.
      Don't let me miss this boat.
I know it should be more than sheer enigma.
    I stand its drink, I hold its coat,
And acquiesce to all its tangled stigma,
      Stigmata, stain,
    But what's the value of sigma?
      What's there to gain
By sacrifice, by self-abasing?
      I'll bear the pain
But let me hear the music that I'm facing.

4. 'I AM THAT I AM'

Always hide-and-seeking, aren't you, God?
    Always on the lam.
    Ever inconceivable. Odd
      To reckon with. 'I am,'
You whisper, unexpected, from a bush
    That burns too brightly, 'that I am.'
Which maybe could assuage us at a push.
      I trusted you.
    But heaven is all cush
      And honeydew,
  Your unrelatable paradise
      Where follow-through
Is fathomless, and purpose imprecise.

5. MEANING

The infinite is habitually subdividing,
    Letting fresh patterns play
    Along the riffed face of its gliding
    Shallows, where pilgrims stray
In hope of finding what seemed often missing:
    Meaning, meaning that greenish-grey
Horizon where outrageous geese go hissing
    And, in the cool
    Showdown of sundown, kissing
    Meteors fool
Across the cirrus-staircased sky,
    And fractals pool
As if to say, 'This light will never die.'

6. MATHEMATICAL PLATONISM

'The number of the wandering stars is seven,'
    The old cosmology said.
    Time overturns some views of heaven.
    But, though that picture's dead,
One possibility it presupposed,
    That numbers aren't just in the head
But actually exist, is not foreclosed:
    And, if they do,
    I do not feel disposed
    To think it true
That this world is the whole shebang.
    We puzzle through.
Perhaps it's why they said the planets sang.

7. ἈΛΉΘΕΙΑ / TRUTH

The 'unforgettable', the song that sticks,
    The earworm in the warm
    Hammer-and-stirrup nest that ticks
    As herald of the storm,
Or ἄγγελος, which turns into our 'angel';
    The final namer of the norm,
Irradiate with the subtleties that change'll
    Never disperse,
    Guarding its moated grange well;
    A kind of hearse
And heaven rolled together. Strewth,
    It could be worse,
Than being at the beck and call of truth.

8. MERIDIAN

As in the Tintin book 'Red Rackham's Treasure'
    They finally realise
    The map works by a different measure.
    The scales fall from their eyes:
Not Greenwich but the Paris Meridian!
    Startled, we learn the lost hoard lies
Below the floorboards where their quest began.
    And so with me –
    The all-consuming plan
    Turns out to be
The glaring one I least suspected,
    Which sets me free
To read the gridlines clearly, be collected.

9. CONSCIOUSNESS

A tiny fly just crawled across the page.
    Is it intelligent?
    Responsive, sure, and did engage
    With the gentle breeze I sent.
But is it 'conscious'? Does it have a 'mind'?
    Do dolphins? Dogs? I'm not content
With thinking all these sadly left behind
    In purgatory.
    Delusional humankind.
    Observably,
    There's passion all along the line,
    Where we can see
Love's mindedness, organic, like a vine.

10. KNOWLEDGE

Knowledge is meant for branching, growing greater,
    Recording what unfolds
    As if by muscle memory, later
    Unleashed, a maze of moulds
With plaster statues rising from dead-ends,
    Pattern divulging what it holds:
A mind's self-shifting, charged to make amends
    By setting free
    The passion that depends
    On tirelessly
Grafting the casual and arcane,
    Growing to be
One bricolage of Lego bricks, a brain.

11. MISSA SOLEMNIS IN D MAJOR

It goes beyond the walls of any building.
    I listen and I feel
    As if the storms of notes were gilding
    The bleary air with real
Stuccoed accretions. Is the infinite
    Perceptible to those who wheel
Within these finite ranges? Is the light,
    The way it blesses,
    A message that we might
    Decode? My guess is
Maybe. And this is why, above
    All noes and yeses,
I turn again to what I will call love.

12. FINDING WORDS

The words of love strike hard when they are soft,
    Sound soft when they are hard.
    Like beachballs buffeted aloft,
    They drift with disregard
For where they started or who sent them flying.
    It's agony to drop your guard,
Live with the conscious knowledge you are dying,
    And find no more
    Than love's intensifying,
    Life's tragic flaw,
Infinity's magnetic parts.
    (The moral law
Has watchful officers in all our hearts.)

13. SUNSET

The gaunt giant bent to kiss the trembling land
    And all the clouds went red.
    How can I begin to understand
      What's in the world's old head?
Does justice oversee this unjust mess?
    I love my life, so I do dread
My death. And I fear pain. And I confess
    I fail to know
    Why all this fallenness
      Shouldn't be so,
    Except that I feel it is no good.
      Please, must I go?
True vine, tell me about the Land of Should.

14. THE LAND OF SHOULD

I would it were a place that we could go,
    If only for a while.
    Then maybe we'd begin to know
      The outcome of this trial,
Or maybe not. I guess the weather's fine
    And lush fruit cluster in the style
Of Caravaggio, murkily divine,
    And, more than that,
    We're kinder there. We line
      The habitat
    With open evenness – too far?
      No, more than that.
A land that sent love as its avatar.

15. ONTOLOGICAL ARGUMENT

Imagine the greatest being there could be.
    But would it not be best
    If more than possibility,
      A wonder somehow blessed
With real existence? 'Then it must be so,'
    Some say, and yes, I can, if pressed,
Half-see it, when I squint: a flawless glow
    Above the haze,
    A knowledge that we know
      By hidden ways
Before we think, remembered maps
      Through the mind's maze,
Which one day will make sense to us perhaps.

16. KNOWING AND NOT KNOWING

Waistcoated know-how of the Belle Époque
    Thought it had sussed all things.
    Elizabethans – taking stock
      Of Pegasus's wings,
Automata, potatoes – had no such
    Illusions: everlasting springs
Of mystery met them everywhere. And much
    Came to be known.
    The knowledge eras clutch
      Is a stepping stone,
    But honour for the ground we tread
      Can't be outgrown.
Humility is endless, someone said.

17. THE FRANTIC

For years I spoke too quickly, was too frantic,
    Too stoked to get things done.
    Always desiring some gigantic
      Denouement. On the run
From stillness and the serenity it brings,
    That sense of resting in the spun
Crib of reality. Yet words have wings
    And when I heard
    (At first reluctant) things
      That seemed absurd
    But twisted in my solar plexus,
      This tired heart stirred
And I began to trace the vine's vast nexus.

18. HOPEFULS

Rainwashed, light's writhing kilters and relapses,
    Wind-flurries, rivets, sticks,
    Like blankly-skittering synapses
      Up to their usual tricks,
Or spiral galaxies sambaing through space.
    We're gawkers at the latest flicks –
Hopefuls suffused with something once called grace,
    Which you might now
    Better describe as a place
      Where why and how
    Throw winks across an old divide,
      And the sacred cow
Says to the sad ones, 'I am on your side.'

19. TO A FRIEND

Reclusive friend, bear with me for a while.
    I couldn't, wouldn't dare
    To sound your feelings, cramp your style,
      Or stand within your glare.
I tend to keep it secret, out of view,
    Our life-affirming love-affair,
Though you must know now, knowing the depths you do,
    How groundingly
    I rest my hopes on you.
      Imagine me
    Imagining you! Some brand it odd,
      And it may be.
But I, notorious friend, will name you, God.

20. MYSTERY

Much like the thief who wore his shoes reversed
    So when he ran away
    His endpoint seemed where he'd been first,
      Jehovah took the grey
Path of obscurity and left us baffled,
    Not knowing, if we die today,
Whether our hard-to-pinpoint souls are raffled
    To take fresh shapes,
    Suddenly cinched and snaffled
      Into ants or apes,
    Or whether there's some waiting room
      With cheese and grapes,
Where a silent angel designates our doom.

21. THE COUNTENANCE

The countenance would countenance it, surely,
    A path of being kind
  And knowing nothing vastly, purely,
    Or perfectly defined,
Except the clobbered lightning rod of good.
   Strange thought. But friend, you know my mind.
Personification is a game that could
    Distract us for
   Too long. There's work we should
    Not now ignore:
  Close purposiveness, which amounts,
    In time, to more.
You say, 'Is this belief?' I say, 'It counts.'

22. A WORD

What I call 'God' is not what some call 'God',
    That's fairly evident.
  Vague thunderer with the staff and rod?
    Far from what I've meant.
I mean to say now's view is not enough.
   Skimming materialism's bent
Nature from all proportion. It is tough
    But we have toyed
Undeeply. More than stuff
    Lost in dead void,
  Love's purpose branches, unconfined,
    Never destroyed,
Through everything, an all-cohering mind.

Revisiting a Christian Poetics

on Michael Edwards

DAVID JASPER

Prayer is one thing, quite another is how
throughout the day I appear to you,
a wise man from the west bearing gifts
of guilt, and frank disobedience, and murmur.
— Michael Edwards, *At the Brasserie Lipp*

The following essay was first read as a paper written for a day conference held at the Maison Française in Oxford on 17 May 2019. Some of its oral qualities have been deliberately retained. The conference was held in honour of the literary scholar Sir Michael Edwards, and specifically to celebrate the publication of his most recent collection of poems At the Brasserie Lipp *(2019). Having been for many years Professor of English and Comparative Literature at the University of Warwick, Edwards became the first English person to be elected to the Académie française in 2013. I am concerned here with Edwards' life-long reflections on the relationship between poetry and Christian theology.*

I DO NOT REMEMBER EXACTLY how many years it is since I first met Michael Edwards, but I think it must be about thirty-five. Certainly it was before 1984, when I bought my copy of his book *Towards and Christian Poetics* almost as soon as it was published in that year. Four years later I bought his subsequent collection of essays on the power of poetic language entitled *Poetry and Possibility* (1988), and the two books continue to reside on my bookshelves, both of them now shabby and bearing the marks of much use.

I have spent most of my professional life since then reflecting upon and doing my best to teach students in the University of Durham and then Glasgow about the relationship between literature and theology, an academic exercise that can never be engaged in properly without some recourse to prayer (whatever we may think that finally is). Nevertheless this should never exonerate us from careful, considered and crafty critical thinking. Indeed, quite the contrary is the case. After decades of engagement in such work (universities today call it being

'interdisciplinary' though I have never been quite sure that I fully understood what that word actually means[1]) I have got to the stage in life when I find myself saying that things are not what they were and I sense that a spark of life that was alight in the 1980s is now dimmed and the study of literature and theology today is somehow lacking in its former imaginative, creative and intellectual energy.

However, when I return now to Michael Edwards' two books of essays of 1984 and 1988 there is certainly no lack of imagination, creativity and intellectual vigour. But there is also something more than these things alone that draws me back to his work, something that is, in the end, more vital and ultimately theological. Here are some of Edwards' words from the first chapter of *Poetry and Possibility*, an essay which is entitled 'Writing Paradise Lost':

---

1 See Stanley Fish's excellent essay "Being Interdisciplinary Is So Very Hard to Do," in *There's No Such Things as Free Speech... and it's a good thing too* (Oxford: Oxford University Press, 1994), pp. 231–42.

The poem is exemplary in that it explores, along with so much else, the problems of writing in a fallen world, and the power of poetry to work towards a renewal of that world; but it is exemplary too in that, while recounting the actual story of that fall and renewal, it places itself, truly and honestly, in the distance between Paradise lost and Paradise regained.[2]

In his works of literary criticism, like his fellow literary scholar, Sir Geoffrey Hill, Edwards remains a poet at heart, his language and grammar being instruments of the finest and sharpest order to express and embrace thought and idea. It is this living language that sustains the life of his reflections on Christian poetics – seeking to articulate something that cannot be too closely or too arrogantly, defined, but *towards* which we reach out, in faith and in the words of critical discourse as they engage with the texts of literature.

I recall a brief exchange between Michael Edwards and myself many years ago at a conference in the University of Leicester. It was during that time in the 1980s when the thought of Jacques Derrida and deconstruction were everyone's lips, and departments of literature seemed to be more interested in developing critical theory than in reading literature itself. I remember Edwards being gently but sharply critical of my then current intellectual enthusiasms in the fields of postmodernity, and his words sent me back to a re-reading of *Towards a Christian Poetics*. My questions and concerns then were (and still are) primarily theological, bearing in mind that I had had two separate and quite distinct experiences of studying as an undergraduate, one concluding with a degree in English and French literature, the other in fairly traditional Christian theology at Oxford. I have never quite been able to bring those two now rather ancient intellectual experiences into focus with one another, a difficulty that has, I might say, continued to stimulate my intellectual and spiritual life ever since. In the early 1980s everything that was embraced within that sprawling term 'literary theory' seemed to bear down with hostile intent upon all other fields of study within the humanities, colonizing, among other things, the field of theology with theoretical devices and desires that were often remote from either literary texts or Christian doctrine. But in a re-reading of the first chapter of *Towards a Christian Poetics* I encountered something rather different that only now, I think, after all these years, I am beginning truly to appreciate.

Those many decades ago, as a second-time undergraduate, I sat in a lecture room in the University of Oxford and heard the then Regius Professor of Divinity, Maurice Wiles (a theologian whose work deserves to be better remembered than it is) speak of theology as a 'second order language.'[3] Let me be quite clear. I firmly believe that a careful, informed and thoughtful theology should accompany the Christian life, but that perhaps at the heart of faithful Christian belief is something else – a

finally unified creative poetics (that, I acknowledge, is almost a tautology) that shapes and enlivens the religious life. In short, we may find ourselves moving towards a Christian poetics with our thought and theology wholly enriched by literature and the language of poetry. Edwards begins an essay on his fellow poet and critic Sir Geoffrey Hill with a reference to Hill's first collection of poetry, *For the Unfallen* (1959). He notes: 'The title… involves wordplay. As quoted from the concluding poem it backhandedly dedicates the book to those who fail to recognise that they are fallen more deeply, and implicated in a fallen world.'[4] In a Christian poetics, also, words are at play less in moments of statement but rather in acts of *implicature* – that is, following the lead of H. P. Grice - instances in language of intentionally implying a meaning which can be inferred from an utterance in conjunction with its conversational or semantic context, but is neither explicitly expressed nor logically entailed by the instance itself.[5]

After this rather crabbed, though I hope still useful, statement, let me return to the more elegant and expressive language of Edwards himself, finding the roots of Christian theology and its pattern of fall and redemption within the chamber of a Christian poetics and in creative critical exchanges with literary texts themselves. I share with Edwards, though from a humble distance, an enthusiasm for the poetry and poetic prose of the French poet Yves Bonnefoy. Of him Edwards has written:

The 'sacred' is one of Bonnefoy's most urgent concerns, though it is envisaged in a purely terrestrial perspective. It is partly the perception of unity, of the gathering of the scattered; a powerful motif, of course, in the poetry of disinheritance, since it only requires a number of phenomena to appear to harmonise for their observer to believe he is glimpsing Eden.[6]

The final image is, of course, highly significant and that glimpse of Paradise is very far from unique in Bonnefoy's poetry. Within the power of words we both fall and then glimpse redemption – theology here implied, present, and awaiting renewal.

In a Christian poetics words are both exact and exacting. A review of *Towards a Christian Poetics* by Bishop Richard Harries in *The Church Times* in 1984 described Edward's style as 'sometimes cryptic'.[7] I do not find that this is the case. It is rather that we have today become so accustomed to language, not least critical language, as utilitarian and stripped down for ease of consumption that a return to the carefully crafted, living word and words is often perceived as a difficulty rather than as a creative challenge. Early in *Towards a Christian Poetics*

---

2 Michael Edwards, *Poetry and Possibility* (London: Macmillan, 1988), p. 21.

3 Wiles' lectures were published in a little book entitled *What is Theology?* (Oxford: Oxford University Press, 1976), which remains valuable reading for all students of the subject.

4 *Poetry and Possibility*, p. 169.

5 For an excellent essay on implicature, see Martin Warner, 'Philosophy, Implicature and Liturgy', in David Jasper and R. C. D. Jasper, Eds. *Language and the Worship of the Church* (London: Macmillan, 1990), pp. 147–73.

6 *Poetry and Possibility*, p. 138.

7 I have not been able to recover a precise date for this review. It remains inserted in in my copy of *Towards a Christian Poetics*, placed there in 1984.

the reader is directed to the great literary forms of trag-edy (the 'dialectic of tragedy') and comedy and to what Edwards calls the craft of story as something that is 'quite mysterious and certainly not to be taken for granted'.[8] But I have elected here to move beyond these early chap-ters of the book to what is perhaps its central discussion, that concerning T. S. Eliot and language. In a chapter that is essentially a conversation with Eliot's poetry, Edwards takes his reader on a Christian journey through the world of the poetry's form and language. We learn to begin with of the 'fall of language' but not merely at second hand and from the sometimes remote distance of a theological narrative. In the act of reading the fall is again experi-enced. Of 'Gerontion' Edwards writes: 'Part of the speak-er's "terror" is that he cannot escape from the maze of his fallen language. Corrupt, he writes a corrupt work.'[9] As readers we enter a dangerous world that is at the same time full of potential salvation, and for Gerontion as for Prufrock 'salvation involves a new language'.[10] Led by the poet (as Virgil leads Dante in *The Divine Comedy*), we fall into the dissonant wasteland of Babel, though even in this dark place, in *The Waste Land*, there is glimpsed in language a possibility that is beyond speech.

> I could not
> Speak, and my eyes failed, I was neither
> Living nor dead, and I knew nothing,
> Looking into the heart of light, the silence.[11]

Of light ,and more particularly of silence, I will say more in a moment. In his chapter on T. S .Eliot Edwards offers us a brief but vital discussion regarding the nature of a Christian poem. Although it is very brief this discussion is, for me, the centre of *Towards a Christian Poetics*, though I find aspects of it, shall we say, challenging, perhaps too allusive in its implications (that word again) for comfort. But perhaps that is deliberate. Edwards writes again:

> A Christian poem should be Christian in itself. But there is another problem. The language of a Christian poem should also be Christian. (As the language of a tragedy should, argu-ably, be tragic.)
>
> The subject is very complex, and has hardly begun to be examined; its implications seem to me to be awesome. Eliot is the writer, I think, who made the essential move. A 'Chris-tian' intuition about language before his conversion led to a poetry enacting the fall of language. *Ash-Wednesday* is an attempt to redeem language.[12]

Language itself is redeemed by the poet's words, the poem being a spiritual exercise in loss and recovery. This chapter on Eliot brings us, inevitably, to *The Four Quar-tets*, and concludes with fragmentary conversations between poets – Shakespeare, Lancelot Andrewes (who was a poet at heart, despite being a bishop, searching for the 'full juice of meaning'[13] in words), Christopher Mar-lowe, Mallarmé and finally Eliot himself. At the very end of this conversation Edwards writes: 'It is not enough to say that Eliot's poems are 'about' language, as other Symbolist works: they are concerned with language as fallen and capable of re-creation; they aggress language, and attempt to remake it.'[14] Thus, in the end, the attempt of language is only fully realized in the Word – the Logos – that was from the beginning, and which both begins and ends in silence. So what, then, in all this play of lan-guage, of the silence that lies at its heart? We turn now to chapter 9 of *Towards a Christian Poetics*, with its title 'Sublunary Music'.

There is, on the one hand, a dark silence of absence and, on the other, there is a light-filled fullness of silence that is the conclusion of all speech and music. As we enter into this latter silence we may be transformed – or is the right word transfigured? – by what Edwards calls a dialectical process, 'whereby a fallen world... of hearing and sometimes of speech, is transformed, and suggests the possibility of a greater and future Transforming. It functions, like any art, between nature and re-creation'.[15] Words and sounds are spoken and carried on the breath that finally breathes into a silence: as Jesus breathes his last word of completion and new beginning on the cross, 'τετελεσται'[16]; as the Spirit in the beginning of all creation, the wind from God, moves across the face of the waters; as Elijah hears the silence of the still small voice. It is known far beyond Christian theology and the Bible in the literature of many cultures. I am reminded, for exam-ple, of the celebrated passage early in T. E. Lawrence's *Seven Pillars of Wisdom*, when Lawrence finds himself led by his Arab escorts into a ruin in North Syria, dating of ancient Roman times, when he:

> drank with open mouth of the effortless, empty, eddyless wind of the desert, throbbing past. The slow breath had been born beyond the distant Euphrates and had dragged its way across many days and nights of dead grass, to its first obsta-cle, the man-made wall of our broken palace. About them it seemed to fret and linger, murmuring its baby-speech. 'This,' they told me, 'is the best: it has no taste.[17]

Words breathe and speak into silence, allowing us to hear, if only for a moment, the divine language, lifting us from our endless daily distractions and chatterings. Perhaps the Middle English word 'janglings' expresses this dissonance more precisely. Michael Edwards again:

> From the moment... that the humans listen to the wrong words – to the words that are wrong – untroubled relation is lost, with God-as-Word, and with the divine word in the uni-

---

8 Michael Edwards, *Towards a Christian Poetics* (London: Macmillan, 1984), p. 72.

9 Ibid. p. 105.

10 Ibid. p. 106.

11 Ibid. p. 108. T. S. Eliot, *The Wasteland*, Part 1, ll. 38–42. *The Poems of T. S. Eliot*. Vol. 1. Ed. Christopher Ricks and Jim McCue (London: Faber & Faber, 2015), p. 56.

12 Ibid. pp. 114–15.

13 Ibid. p. 128.

14 Ibid. p. 128.

15 Ibid. p. 200.

16 Gospel of John 19: 30.

17 T. E. Lawrence, *Seven Pillars of Wisdom: A Triumph*. Vol. 1. (London: World Books, 1939), p. 38.

verse and in men. Yet the language of God remains literally vital, a nourisher of life, as Jesus describes it in the Gospels: 'It is written, Man shall not live by bread alone, but by every word that proceedeth out of the mouth of God' (Matthew 4: 4).[18]

The poetic vocation, like the priestly (I speak as a priest myself, though I am no poet), is then profoundly theological, but in a creative way that the theologians of the Christian Church too often miss. In my years of trying to teach theology and literature in a university setting I have never felt entirely comfortable with the growth of what is now called 'Practical Theology' – born it often seems to me of too great an anxiety to be seen to be useful in some way. But true theology must begin in acts of praise and celebration, in worship and contemplation and belief, and these may grow into a poetics that is itself, in its very substance and being, theological and perhaps Christian. Edwards writes, with characteristic carefulness and clarity, of the non-Christian poet Charles Tomlinson:

> Seeing, according to the title of Tomlinson's first full-length collection, is believing, but hasn't his point been missed? Not only is this more than a demand for evidence: the stress falls quite as much on the believing as on the seeing, for the adage has been sounded and then reversed. It declares, surely, in the light of the poems that follow, that what is achieved in seeing well is a kind of belief.[19]

There is far more that may be said of Edward's two books, *Towards a Christian Poetics* and *Poetry and Possibility*, than I can possibly manage in these few rather fragmentary remarks. There are poets, mainly English or French, with whom Edwards exchanges reflections on the power and mystery of words that have not here been mentioned – Milton, Wordsworth, Hopkins, Hardy, Baudelaire, Marianne Moore, and many others. He addresses also the question of translation and its deep poetic mystery in conversations both within and beyond language itself. (During my years of teaching in China I was often told that the most sensitive modern translator of Chinese poetry into English was Ezra Pound, though he knew hardly any Mandarin.) Edwards offers to his reader reflections on music and visual art, thoughts upon the multilingual work *Renga*, and adapting Japanese poetic forms to Western poetry. But above all, for me, there is the sense throughout his writings of the Spirit at work in the words of the poet, upsetting what Edwards has called Derridean complacency and reaching towards and sometimes into the mysterious heart of a Christian poetics. So let me conclude with the closing words of *Towards a Christian Poetics* (which the Church of England might have done well to heed as it set out its dry linguistic priorities for its liturgy now known as *Common Worship*):

> Our words, being fallen, are no longer capable of addressing God correctly, and our breath is that of a body 'subjected to vanity'. So a greater language inhabits us, that of the Spirit, or of the Breath itself. The limits of our world, defined, according to Wittgenstein, by the limits of our language, are transcended by a language that has no limits – by the divine language, itself dialectical, which, having given us life and preserving us in death, groans towards resurrection.[20]

> And then, perhaps, our words, wrought in our present Babel of tongues, will find themselves transfigured into the unity and the silence of the Word, which is the heart of God.

---

18 *Towards a Christian Poetics*, p. 219.
19 Ibid. p. 154.

20 Ibid. p. 237.

From the Archive

Issue 150, March–April 2003

SINÉAD MORRISSEY

Fellow contributors to this issue include Paul Muldoon, Carola Luther, Andrew Motion, Les Murray and Jane Yeh.

from ON OMITTING THE WORD 'JUST' FROM MY VOCABULARY

And here I am in a room I don't recognise, being
angular and contemporary, with its own
unabashed light source and the table clear.

I must be somewhere Scandinavian.
Where weather is decisively one way
or the other, and summer,

or winter, will not brook contradiction.
Even the ornaments (such as they are)
are purposeful: a stone dog stares into the fireplace

as though pitting itself against fire
for the next quarter-century.

Two Poems

YU XIUHUA

Translated by Wang Fang and Yvonne Reddick

Confession of Love

I try hard at life: I carry water, cook, and take all my pills on time.
I throw myself into it, like putting a piece of dried orange peel in my tea when the sun is warm and bright.
I drink my different teas in turn: chrysanthemum, jasmine, rose and lemon –
all these lovely things bring me to the path that leads to spring.
So again and again I press down the snow in my heart –
it's too pure and close to spring.
I read your poems in a clean yard. All the world's love-affairs
are a blur, like sparrows darting by,
and the years are pure as moonlight. No, I'm not being sentimental –
if I send you a book, it won't be poetry.
I'll send you a book about plants and crops,
telling you the difference between rice and grass,
telling you how the grasses that look like rice are afraid of spring.

My Dog Xiaowu

I limped out of the yard: she trotted at my heels.
We passed the vegetable patch and the furrowed fields to go north to my grandma's.
When I stumbled and fell in a ditch, she wagged her tail –
I stretched out my hands, and she licked the blood to clean them.

He was drunk, and he said that there was a girl in Beijing
better-looking than me. They go dancing on their days off.
He likes girls who dance –
he loves watching them shake their bottoms.
He says they always moan and groan in bed – it really turns him on –
not like me: I'm always silent, I even cover my face.

I ate in silence.
I called 'Xiaowu, Xiaowu' and threw her some meat.
She wagged her tail, barking with joy.

All those times he pulled my hair and banged my head against the wall –
Xiaowu wagged her tail.
He was powerless to hurt a woman with no fear of pain.

When we got to grandma's house,
we realized that she'd been dead for years.

Xiaowu (小巫) means 'little witch' in Chinese.

Two Poems

SUJATA BHATT

A Neutral Country

He just wanted to step out
for a walk – some fresh air
to clear his head – and on the way back
he told his wife, he'd get some milk and eggs.
But he found dead bodies in front of his door,
five dead bodies, all young, all so young,
he repeats. It will take him a long time
to recover from this.
Now he prefers to stay at home.

*

One day a letter arrives,
an invitation, we accept –
We agree to visit a neutral country.

We cross rivers and valleys and mountains.
It is a quiet journey.
A strange brightness surrounds us.

*

Over here the air smells of cheese.
The first light in the morning
comes through layers of fog.

White gauze – endless veils –

And somewhere along the paths
we cannot see, somewhere, they tell us
Psyche walks, Eurydice walks –

They want us to believe –

We know there are cows somewhere
                and church bells
waiting to be heard – But now
even the grapes are asleep.

*

They let us stay in one of their castles
and ask us to entertain their King.

Their King arrives with apples and honey,
        with chocolate and coffee.
Their King arrives with a violin
        and bottles of wine.

We never know what to say to him
and listen to his stories instead.

*

It's a castle protected by roses,
a castle protected by a lake.

Their lake smells of the dreams of birds –
there are dreams they call ghosts
and dreams they call fish.

Somehow they know what birds believe.

Their fish are alive and smell of nothing.
The lake's water smells of winter –
as if winter breathes within it.

The lake's water holds the memory
of a silver necklace once forgotten in the grass –

*

Afternoons we sit in their rose garden
and watch bees follow the sun.
Their roses are so fragrant
our hearts ache – our hearts ache
and we do not know why.

We watch lizards turn into leaves
and leaves turn into lizards.
We listen to the soft scraping, rustling sound
of their flight as they race down
the steps of the castle.
Even the oldest, most beautiful stones
cannot keep them.

But a nun follows the lizards
to a graveyard – and there she sings
to them until they dance.
She shows us how she does this
day after day – and we watch the way she turns
towards the roses.

*

It is August, early August –
before sundown –
        and as we walk through
                their vineyards
we can feel shadows turn gold.

*

We have forgotten to count the days,
forgotten why we came here.

They ask us to look at the stars,
at the moon – they ask us to believe –

The Swan Princess Speaks

Because I found myself alone
in a cold, dark country, my mother long dead,
my father murdered, my brothers driven far away,
far beyond rivers and mountains I knew—
because I found myself alone
I wanted to be everything:
a girl and a swan. I wanted to be free
to fly anywhere, to be a bird at home in any land,
at home on water and in the air.
I dreamed a world where water lilies
guide me. Fish glisten, sliding through deeper shadows.
Wind-entangled light surrounds me.
I asked the sun to give me strength,
the moon, to heal my soul. I learned to sing
the language of the stars.
And so I lived as a girl and a swan.
I grew stronger. I searched for my brothers.
Do not ask me to say more,
this is enough for today.

NOTE: This poem was commissioned by The Poetry Society as part of *Art Russe, The Art of Story-telling*. It was inspired by Mikhail Vrubel's painting 'The Swan Princess' and displayed as part of an exhibition at the Mall Gallery, London.

A Deed of Quixote

HORATIO MORPURGO

'Can you give me any idea when my Don Quixote will be published?
You have had the typescript two years now and I feel that the time must be coming near...'
— J. M. (John Michael) Cohen to Alan Glover, November 1949

THE TENTH PENGUIN CLASSIC finally appeared in 1950, over-budget and late. A rise in the price of paper had held up publication. Sales of the 950-page seventeenth-century Spanish novel were, to begin with, slow. A nervous letter to the overall editor of the series reported, a year later, that the book had hardly begun to break even. Should we be surprised then that neither this *Quixote* nor its translator figures much in the way we remember post-war British culture?

I think we should be surprised. J.M. Cohen would refer to himself, a few years later, as a 'translation factory', which was no exaggeration. By 1955 he was simultaneously at work on *The Life of Saint Teresa by Herself*, a selection from Montaigne's *Essays* and *The Penguin Anthology of Spanish Verse*. His editor, Alan Glover, joked with him that before long he would be 'the only Classics translator'. He was 'special editorial consultant' to the series as a whole. He originated and ran the 'European Poets' list within it, offering bilingual selections of Rilke, Hölderlin, Lorca, Pushkin and others.

As for his *Don Quixote*, Thornton Wilder soon wrote in to say 'I shall leave Harvard with the emphatic injunction that henceforth your text is used' and there were other big orders from American universities. After that slow start it went on to sell more than 300,000 copies and remained in print for half a century. When Cohen sent in his two specimen chapters in 1945 and was commissioned on the strength of them to translate the whole novel, Penguin was making one of those excellent early decisions on which its reputation was built. His contribution is not in doubt.

Why then do we hear so little about him? The reasons are several. One was his own modesty, which we'll come to. Another reason is that his achievement stands at a slight angle to the story we most often tell ourselves about post-war Britain. To translate from Spanish to English was and is to translate from one living global language into another. As we'll see, doing so led Cohen well beyond the bounds of Europe in any territorial sense.

The story we tell ourselves: E.V. Rieu's is, rightly, the name most closely identified with the beginnings of the Classics. Invited in 1944 to set the series up, he began at once to seek out translators 'from the Greek, Latin and later European languages'. Of his own best-selling *Odyssey* (1946), the first of the series, he later wrote that he had turned to Homer from 'a world of fantastically distorted values'. The revision of his text 'was undertaken to the sound of V1 and V2 explosions and the crash of shattering glass'. That the series began with this epic tale of a hero's return from war only appeared to confirm the overall impression. The Classics were an intellectual counterpart to the rebuilding of bombed-out cities, a re-affirmation of the shattered European collective.

This account is due a closer look. It's not wrong – indeed, if any part of the series can be said to have picked up the hard-hat of post-war reconstruction, it was Cohen's own European Poets. But the narrative does need qualifying. Rieu actually began his translation of the *Odyssey* before the war and long before the Classics were ever thought of. The early Classics are uneven in their Europhilia – the first one translated from Latin, *Tacitus on Britain and Germany* (1948), describes the inhabitants of the latter as 'a people who had already begun to become a European problem in the 1st century of our era'.

Day-to-day running of the series was not, in any case, in Rieu's hands. It was left to that 'unacknowledged genius of Penguin' whom we've already met, Alan Glover. Rieu liked Cohen's style and said so, or gave it 'a high adjective of praise' as Glover teasingly put it. But Glover and Cohen were more than colleagues. A letter of Cohen's records a drink they went for not long after the launch of *Don Quixote*. It's clear they have been talking mainly about fourteenth-century German mystics and have had a terrific time. The two were soon firm friends. They might have little enough in common by background but they more than made up for it in other ways.

Glover was older and without university education. Imprisoned as a conscientious objector during the First World War, he had taught himself Russian, Greek and Sanskrit in a number of prisons. His face and hands were scarred by the marks of excised tattoos from his years as a circus 'tattoo man'. Cohen was a Cambridge graduate turned autodidact, Ishmael to Glover's Queequeg. After university he went to work in the family furniture business and learnt Spanish during the 1930s. He taught himself Russian on commuter trains whilst working as a teacher during the Second World War. His background was Jewish agnostic while Glover had been a Quaker and a Franciscan tertiary. Both, by the time they met, were deeply read in Buddhist literature. To read their correspondence is to watch the recondite allusions and risqué commentary shuttling merrily back and forth.

Cohen was soon relying on Penguin for much of his income: he was the freelance, Glover the editor. The shared humour and taste for abstruse learning served to smooth over whatever awkwardness there might have been. Owing to the delays, for example, *Don Quixote* eventually went on sale at a higher cover price than had been assumed by the original contract. Part of what Cohen was owed therefore fell due sooner than anticipated. When Glover promptly paid up, Cohen, with children to feed, thanked him for 'a deed of Quixote in a world of Fabians'. The term 'Fabians' here is used consciously in a double sense, referring both to Penguin's left-wing ethos and to the Roman commander famous for his 'delaying tactics'.

Cohen wasted no time, as we've seen, making himself indispensable. His communications with Glover suggest not only a personal liking and a shared sense of humour but something like a shared life-project too. When Cohen, asked in 1951 for a bio-note, replies with a send-up of self-promotional puffery, Glover both tells him to quit clowning and continues their joke at the wider culture's expense: 'Penguin-readers are very serious-minded and learned young men and women in quest of truth and the elusive light of pure intellectual satisfaction. If they thought we were not perfectly serious, their faith in human nature would suffer a severe shock. You must remember that the new generation is not like our own. It doesn't drink, it doesn't smoke and it is existentialist. God be praised it will all be destroyed by an atom bomb in a very short time.'

A year or two later, in another bio-note, Cohen revealed that his 'hobby, largely unpractised, is to travel and make contact with his fellow men of letters abroad'. This was a comment with some hinterland to it, as Glover would have been aware. For browsing through the Penguin archive in Bristol, you do now and then find these two having to contain some irritation with each other. Especially over this ticklish question of travel.

By February 1952, Cohen had completed his next translation, Rousseau's *Confessions*. His anthology of *Comic and Curious Verse*, prepared in the course of that year, was turning out to be a Christmas hit when he welcomed, in December, another big commission: to translate Rabelais' *Gargantua and Pantagruel*. Two days later he wrote to Glover, breezily announcing his intention to travel by cargo boat to South America, taking Rabelais with him. 'I am collecting therefore commissions to be done in Buenos Aires...'

There follows a dramatic dropping off in the tone and frequency of their communications. 'Sorry for my slow response,' Glover replies at the end of the month, almost three weeks later. He is recovering, he says, 'partly from the shock of paying my Christmas bills, and partly from the news which your letter conveyed. I have thought hard but fear there is no way we could connect up with your proposed trip.'

'Shock'. 'Fear'. 'Proposed'. There is another pause before Cohen replies: 'I have left your letter of the old year unanswered as my trip has been in process of development.' He follows with more detail on his 'forthcoming' (not 'proposed') trip aboard a brand-new cargo ship, the *Romney*. 'I hope this little adventure of yours,' Glover answers, 'is as successful as you want it to be and that you will come back with the whole of Rabelais nicely typed in your luggage.' Cohen can confirm that he will be lecturing for the British Council and hopes that Penguin's export department will have copies of his *Don Quixote* in the bookshops there.

The defeat of Republican Spain turned many of its intellectuals into exiles, often 'transplanting' them to Latin America. Cohen knew several of these from contacts made in England so he had introductions and somewhere to stay. He evidently hoped also to use his status as translator of the most famous Spanish book to gain entrance to Latin American literary life. Glover missed how canny a move this was but Cohen had reason to trust his instinct and British publishing would one day have cause to be thankful. He had shown this kind of foresight before. His self-taught Russian had borne fruit in a justly celebrated 1946 translation (the first) of Boris Pasternak's poetry into English. With the later publication of *Doctor Zhivago*, the Nobel prize and Pasternak's mistreatment by the Soviet authorities, Cohen's translations were widely reprinted.

So it turned out with this latest 'little adventure'. Its timing could hardly have been luckier. Also working at the British Council in Buenos Aires in 1953 was a certain Jorge Luis Borges. The writer, then in disgrace with Perón's right-wing populist regime, was living in constant fear of arrest. The new government had sacked him from his post as director of a municipal library, offering him a job instead as an inspector of poultry.

The British Council found him more congenial work as a lecturer and it was there that Cohen first met 'the father, the "Great Inca" of the modern Spanish American novel'. He accompanied him on one of his famous rambles around the city. What is not surprising about their conversation is that Cohen, as he recorded it twenty years later, asked Borges about Argentinian writers and was given names. Cohen would come to act as a kind of liaison between the emergent literatures of South America and London publishers. He did not return with Rabelais neatly typed in his suitcase, but he did come back with a typescript of Borges's *El Aleph*, for which he was at that time unable to find a British publisher.

But there is another and more surprising way in which all this relates directly to Penguin Classics and what was behind them. The little book which Cohen wrote about Borges many years later includes his most sustained meditation on what a 'classic' is or might be. Those who ran the series appear to have taken the term as more or less of a common sense one, describing any book 'that has been around for a while and deserves to be taken seriously'. But something was surely lost in all that English understatement. The discussions about translation trod very cautiously around the question of what a classic is.

Others, elsewhere, had dived right in. For a translator from Spanish and French, and especially a translator of *Don Quixote*, wandering round Buenos Aires in the company of Jorge Luis Borges would have had a very special resonance. Borges' *Pierre Menard, Author of the Quixote*, tells the story of a modern Frenchman seeking to 're-write *Don Quixote*'. He cannot 'become a Catholic, fight the Moors and the Turks' or 'forget all of European history between 1602 and the moment of his writing'. Menard in any case has conceived a very different idea – to write the book afresh *in identical words*, as if he himself had written it.

Cohen suggests that this story's core insight is that some such re-writing is what every reader does when he or she reads a classic: 'He reads it with all the centuries' agglomeration of changed view-points and historical experiences,' by which 'he is often tempted... to expand or alter the text.' A contemporary reader always invests the text 'with the altered values of his own time'.

This is what Borges meant when he describes Menard's text as 'verbally identical' but 'almost infinitely richer', enriched with new ambiguities. Menard's style is archaic, it 'suffers from a certain affectation'. Cervantes for his part merely handled with ease the Spanish of his time. Menard 'multiplied draft upon draft, revised tenaciously and tore up thousands of manuscript pages' in the

process. His 'final *Quixote*' is 'a kind of palimpsest, through which the traces... of our friend's "previous" writing should be translucently visible'.

This is as close as any of those centrally involved with the Classics series ever came to articulating why it mattered. Betty Radice, who succeeded Rieu as overall editor, resisted all explanation: 'When asked how I plan the series, my simple answer is that I don't. I muddle along hoping for the best.' But that answer reduces the question to an administrative one. Allen Lane, the company's founding director, was not so shy. The Classics, he speculated, had arisen from Rieu's 'theory, which I think is absolutely right, that each generation really deserves to have the great books of the world in a contemporary idiom'.

Lane / Rieu at least attempt the larger question. But each generation, Borges seems to be saying, and Cohen seems to be agreeing, actually *re-writes* the classics *as it re-reads* them, thereby enriching them with fresh experience. So it isn't only the public that is enriched by this. To set such works before the public was to participate in that longer process, over centuries and millennia, by which the *works themselves* become richer.

Cohen wrote elsewhere of how *Don Quixote* had been continuously 'remade' in this way. Cervantes of course repeatedly insists that his novel is itself a translation from Arabic, the work of a 'wise Muslim philosopher' which he is merely turning into Spanish. Its first translator into English, Thomas Shelton, was an Irishman working even before the second half of the novel had been written. Cohen confessed to having borrowed from him. He had also studied eighteenth- and nineteenth-century versions, observing how each century had read itself into the work. He compared his own 1950 solution to Sancho's speech about his 'wealth' (of proverbial knowledge) with that of a Victorian predecessor. Cohen's version it was that made the novel available to Graham Greene. The result, *Monsignor Quixote* (1989), was a meditation on the exhausted faiths of Communism and Catholicism, both by then having to face their own thoroughly twentieth-century failings. Salman Rushdie has described his own re-imagined *Quichotte* (2019) as 'deranged by his constant exposure to the junk culture of today'.

From his reading of Borges, as from his translation of Cervantes, it's clear that for Cohen the project of transmitting the Classics to the present was neither a narrowly European nor a self-consciously post-war project. Rather, he inscribed his work as an English translator into a tradition stretching back to the sixteenth century and beyond. What had begun as the efforts of a backward European province to keep up with its neighbours now found itself addressing a global audience.

The new fiction in Spanish from Latin America mirrored this tension. Franco's victory had already dented the old country's prestige and a generation went without European pilgrimages during the Thirties and Forties. Maybe it did them good to be thrown back on their own resources, but they were torn. Borges championed, now, a native Argentina that was 'the land of born exiles', or now he declared 'I believe Europe is our tradition'. Through his writing he found some way to live with and use this contradiction.

Some such contradiction has by now long since gone

global. It is one we are all living with, in Europe as elsewhere, some more creatively than others.

Besides his translation work and the anthologies of this new literature, he found other ways to assist in bringing the two continents closer. One story is well known. It was Cohen who, having recently returned from a trip to Mexico, was asked by Tom Maschler, the director of Jonathan Cape, if he knew of any new books there that might find an audience in Britain. Cohen's suggestion was *One Hundred Years of Solitude* by Gabriel Garcia Marquez.

Other stories are less well known. Cohen became, during the 1960s, through his translation of historical works, chief interpreter to the English-speaking world of Spain's (i.e. Europe's) earliest encounter with the Americas. Columbus's *Voyages* and first contact, Cortes and *The Conquest of New Spain*, Pizarro in Peru, later expeditions to the Amazon basin – each of these, for several decades, was best known to the Anglosphere through Cohen's 'translation factory'. But so was that modernist meditation on Teotihuacan, 'Hymn Among Ruins', by Mexican poet Octavio Paz. Cohen's was the first popular translation of Saint Teresa's autobiography. 'Teresa's Vocation', by the modern Cuban poet Belkis Cuza Malé, found its English audience by the same route. Both of these 'remakings' of older stories appeared in anthologies edited by Cohen.

He was invited in 1965, with Allen Ginsberg and others, to judge a literary prize in Cuba and in his *Writers of the New Cuba* (1967) described the experience. He found a similar tension, as in Argentina, between 'criollismo' and Afro-Cuban poetry on the one hand, and Europe, again, on the other. But parallels with his early work on Pasternak must also have suggested themselves. As with Russia earlier in the century, so in Cuba in 1959–60, revolutionary turmoil had produced 'a literary revival, intense but short-lived'. He added an uneasy note at the end of the book about the difficulties already being experienced by 'non-revolutionary writers'.

One of the poems he translated and included was a sequence from 'The Childhood of William Blake' by Heberto Padilla. Blake was a life-long fascination of Cohen's so his interest in this work by a Cuban writer is unsurprising. Padilla had been a strong supporter of the revolution and was a popular writer in a country where literature was a passion. But he had come to have doubts about the direction the revolution had taken. In 1968, Cohen was again in Havana to judge another literary prize. The poetry award went to Padilla but the Government then put pressure on the Union of Writers to condemn the work. When Padilla was imprisoned in 1973 and his cause taken up by the likes of Jean-Paul Sartre and Susan Sontag, Cohen translated a selection of his work for André Deutsch.

'He would like,' read another of his bio-notes, 'to think of himself as one of the last generation of *polymaths*: of those, that is, who know a certain amount about a variety of subjects.' Some expected Cohen to succeed Rieu as overall series editor but it was not to be. From the late Sixties new commissions from Penguin were rare but he remained committed to the company and to the Classics series. It's as if he even found a freedom to explore now the kind of specialist themes unsuited anyway to a mass-market paperback publisher. He did, though, go on asking. In the 1970s he suggested an anthology of Persian poetry, for example. It wasn't the first time they had said no. He had once asked Glover if he could edit a selection of the Metaphysical poets. The early letter already mentioned suggests half-jokingly a selection from Meister Eckhart and Johannes Tauler. Neither of these ever happened.

The deep interest in religion long pre-dated his involvement with Penguin. Once you become aware of this side to him you start seeing it everywhere. A form of meditation that Edward Fitzgerald learnt from the Sufis (Cohen had edited Fitzgerald's letters) was passed to his friend Tennyson, who put it into a poem ('The Flower'), which was read by Borges, and put into a story ('The Zahir'). Saint Teresa's mystical theory is compared with the teachings of the Buddhist Sage Patanjali. A Hindu teacher finds deep affinities between the writings of Meister Eckhart and the Vedanta. As with his Latin American work, attempts to contain what he did within a strictly European frame quickly run into cargo boats departing for Buenos Aires.

This kind of range is not untypical of those who built the Classics series. In 1957 Glover was trying to think up 'a nice new colour' for Classics translated from Pali. Two years *later* it is being acknowledged that 'German literature is very badly represented' on the list, while another 1959 memo reads, 'We want very much to include some Chinese and Japanese classics'. Cohen was editing his European Poets series when he was asked to read specimen chapters of a new translation of the Koran (by N.R. Dawood, then a stateless Iraqi). He approved its 'extremely lucid English'. Glover then wrote to the Home Office – Dawood's residence permit was about to expire – pointing out that he was needed in Britain to complete the translation.

'English', Cohen later wrote, 'has become and remains the common cultural heritage of a vast section of the world.' But the 'universalism' underlying this was, for him at least, more than a function of English-as-global-lingua-franca. The kind of books he was able to write later in life are a useful guide here. *The Common Experience* (1978), for example, is a book about mystical experience, as recorded in secular societies which no longer have any shared language for it, through to that achieved by the most disciplined religious adepts, past and present, east and west.

He wrote it with a former monk, J-F. Phipps, and it includes testimony collected by the Religious Experience Research Unit. But it traces too 'the humanising influence of the Sufis' that was transmitted to Europe, inspiring there the cult of courtly love and the troubadour lyric. It finds 'pleasing resemblances' between Hasidic tales and Zen teachings. To read it now is to be transported to a world vastly removed from that 'clash of civilisations' which has taken such disastrous hold on so many imaginations since.

If the project of post-war European reconstruction hardly seems to have consciously figured at all, that is maybe because the project then had a different name. For there is another project of those years which is implicit everywhere in his writings and in the Penguin archive. Allen Lane singled out the Classics as his proudest achievement in a 1958 interview. And when asked what had pleased him most about the company as a whole, he replied: 'We have made our point that a man who may be poor financially is not necessarily poor in intellectual qualities.' Penguin, he went on, was doing with books 'what Marks and Spencer's has done in clothes and other goods'.

There is nothing to suggest that that second remark was intended ironically. He said this or something very like it several times. Great literature, like well-made clothes, should be available to as many as possible. It was upon a social democratic consensus that the Classics series was built. In so far as that consensus was (Western) Europe-wide, so the project was indeed 'European', even if that is not how they put it. Cohen sees the boom in translation to which he has contributed as 'striving to satisfy the vastly increased public which has remained at school till the age of eighteen, or has taken university courses in non-linguistic subjects'. The stripped-back style of the new translators is for 'a reader in the train or on a holiday beach'.

This is of a piece with his writing on other themes. The new writing in Latin America had found its voice by addressing the 'slowly growing educated middle-class in their own countries'. Four centuries earlier, Elizabethan translations had been 'designed for the ever increasing middle-class which had no knowledge of the original tongues, but a great curiosity'. And so too the Penguin Classics were aimed at the beneficiaries, wherever they were, of the social democratic consensus.

For all that, some of the underlying assumptions about the series are unmistakably conservative. The Senior Common Room atmosphere of the Cohen-Glover correspondence is a case in point. The Classics were 'kinda subversive, kinda hegemonic' as someone cleverly put it. They took a pre-war culture and aimed to make it more widely available. What's astonishing now is that that pre-war idea was available for re-use almost at once. That idea seems to have been hardly if at all damaged by the bombing. Britain had, of course, avoided the trauma of occupation but the story goes back further than that. The success of this series occurred where two rivers joined and both had their sources in a world that long predated the mid-twentieth century crisis.

Culture liberates us from 'systems and system-makers', Mathew Arnold had written in the 1870s. It does so by turning 'a stream of fresh and free thought upon our stock notions and habits'. Arnold spoke for a long-standing liberal faith in the permanent value of certain literary works. He spoke, too, as the son of public-school headmaster. Knowledge of these works was what an education had once transmitted to those lucky enough to receive one. As the welfare state was now expected to redistribute social goods more equitably, so this knowledge, available previously to a few, was now akin to something more like a birth right, a 'share in the great inheritance'.

The other river was a tradition of working-class autodidacts that also went back a very long way. It had been autodidacts, often artisans, who first drove the translation of scripture into English and challenged monopolistic claims to interpret it. It is not irrelevant that both Penguin's founder and one of his closest associates at the company, W.E. Williams (also founder of the Arts Council), had dissenting backgrounds (Methodist and Congregationalist, respectively).

This autodidactic tradition, running on through the eighteenth and nineteenth centuries as Jonathan Rose has shown, burst upon the mid-twentieth century with apparently irresistible force, lifting Penguin, the Left Book Club and others like them as its moment arose. Cohen combined educational privilege with an autodidactic streak and a left-wing outlook. His son Mark recalls him being especially pleased when his selection from Montaigne's *Essays* was chosen as a set text by the Open University. The times were propitious; he belonged to a culture that knew how to use someone like him. We know from his gossiping with Glover how articulate, irreverent and limitlessly curious that culture could be. But a deep and shared seriousness underwrote it. Cohen's address at Glover's funeral quoted from a new translation of the Bhagavad Gita, added to the list only four years earlier.

Back in 1955, with the translation factory already at full capacity, Glover asked Cohen to compile a *Penguin Book of Quotations* – 'Here is an idea to keep you busy for the rest of your life.' He took the work on and completed it over the next three years with Mark's help. In a short memoir, Mark has written of his father that he liked to say he was 'not a great purveyor of my "life and miracles"'. When I asked what that meant, he told me it was a jokey reference to 'people who bragged about their achievements... He was pretty modest about his work and its range'.

You have some idea by now of the range involved. I suggested at the beginning that old-fashioned modesty may have played a part in his being overlooked. It's also what makes his approach so intriguing to a world in which frenetic self-promotion is presented as a minimum requirement for literary-lifers. That it does nobody any good, least of all the lifers, ought to be pretty apparent. Literature, it turns out, got along perfectly well without it.

I expect that modesty was derived from a confidence, though – in his own abilities but not only that. They felt themselves entrusted with a great tradition and called upon to leaven, with it, that great lump which is any mass-consumer society. Perhaps we know better now than to meddle with such high hopes, but I wonder if the scale of that hope did not tend to correct overblown estimates of one's own personal significance.

His world was one in which the language of public life found itself still answerable to language that had stubbornly gone on holding itself to higher standards. Khrushchev and Perón and Castro were, reluctantly, made answerable to the likes of Pasternak and Borges and Padilla. People everywhere, consequently, needed to know what Pasternak and Borges and Padilla had said.

Plus they were curious anyway. It does us no harm to be reminded occasionally of how much has been lost.

Man, image-laden tree,
Words that are flowers, that are fruit, that are deeds.
– Octavio Paz, Hymn Among Ruins, 1948,
translated by J.M. Cohen

*

Special thanks to Mark Cohen, to Penguin Books and to Hannah Lowery at the Penguin Archive in Bristol. Insights from Robert Crowe's 2012 PhD thesis 'Democratising the Classics' (Bristol) are gratefully acknowledged.

from *Hammersmith*

SEAN O'BRIEN

Canto IX

It is far away, sixty years later.
This dying city's leaking steam
From every joint. The libraries are closed,

The discards burning in the mayoral hearth,
And out along the ragged edge
The book of January is white at dawn

Like the long field under hoarfrost
That divides this old estate
On which no library ever stood

And where the poor are exiled now.
To ignorance and rickets.
You cannat eat a poem, canny lad.

Past the full, the tall moon
Climbs aboard its long farewell,
And from the coldest depths

A dog might hear the peal of star-clouds
In the moment of extinction.
At this late stage we find

A promise in these distant facts
When scale must serve for sacrament.
And after all, this book of January

Remains unwritten, does it not?
Why should its pages not record
The works and days of hands like these

Before they perish from the earth?
Here come the early walkers now
To vanish down desire paths

Across the clear, new-published
Whiteness, with white voices raised
As if this field of tall, enormous cold

Was once upon a time a chamber
Where the poor could get a hearing
In a parliament of frost, with words

That might bear scrutiny,
And even now, without recourse,
Perhaps not even memory itself,

They keep a kind of faith
With rumours of a Silver Age
By shouting as they meet and part

And disappear. Ten minutes
See them on their way
From zero hours to graveyard shift.

If they would truly wish it still,
Beyond the habit of forgetfulness
There is another story to be told.

And yet. And yet the book of January
Is having none of it.
I am a text whose only page

Is white, it says. *I am a book of breath,*
That freezes for a moment and is gone.
I've spent my life accumulating books

I now discard for want of space –
Or maybe inclination, since that faith
Seems founded on the air in which it melts.

And yet it's cold, and men once more
Become the wolves they always were.
Juno, Joxer, after '47, after '63,

You would think this is scarcely a winter at all,
But it bites, till the spirit considers itself
An illusion bred out of a settlement

None but the powerless believe in now.
There are people, if you can believe them,
Who think it is nostalgia saying so,

And that we have no history,
And by the logic of their frankness, they
Themselves are scarcely there: cold weather

Thins them down until you see straight through
To the graveyard they will build on next.
Juno and Joxer, tell me: what am I

Contracted to except the past, the solitudes
I cross in search of you? What am I but the tale
You did not think that you were telling?

Canto X

At the end of the garden runs a river
I will never reach. They walk there
In the silence of the intimate, and with the day

So vast and patient they have nothing on the clock.
I come indoors and light the fire
And look up at the flickering leer

On the face of Silenus carved over the mantel.
The old are sent here from the future
To ensure that we despair.

Better never to have been, but failing that
Stick to aesthetics, which in turn
Will stick to you like napalm. Thus Ryan.

Deep beneath the hearth a beam is smouldering,
Ignited by a memory that leaves the city
Mined with unexploded ordnance

Sunk among the bones in flooded graves.
Re-reading Captain January and Braddock by the fire
I am part, still, of the done war.

The old weight-bearing beam consumes itself
Austerely, by the splinter, in a steady, tended rage
Whose day will come and look like vindication

When the stack of storeys falls into itself
And through itself, and down again
And down, through the final dark river to nowhere,

For underneath this fury that will seek
Its own extinction in the wreck
Of all that stands and call it victory,

There is no bedrock to be found.
Imaginary England
Rises for a moment like a gas-flare

From a sewer and is gone.
Now leave me with the house divided
To await its immolation, to bear witness here,

Complicit by the fact of being born
And drinking from the poisoned well.
Let books and earth and oily water burn,

Likewise the living and the dead,
But let me remember the possible days,
The river, where the garden ends

And those I lost are walking still.

'For in the moment I saw you, you were changed'

The American Pastoral of Douglas Crase

IAN POPLE

THE POETRY OF DOUGLAS CRASE is not very extensive. It is limited to a single book length volume, *The Revisionist,* published by Little, Brown in 1981, and an eighteen-page pamphlet/chapbook, *The Astropastorals,* published by Pressed Wafer in 2017. In a note appended to that pamphlet, Crase comments of its contents, 'The last to appear, 'Astropastoral', was published in 2000'. Such a note might suggest that, for all intents and purposes, Douglas Crase has stopped writing poetry. In February of 2018, Pressed Wafer published Crase's 'essays and addresses' in a volume entitled *Lines from London Terrace.*

The appearance of the two new books has given commentators the opportunity to pay Crase's writing attention, after some thirty-seven years of near neglect. The neglect followed the thunderous ovation which *The Revisionist* received on its appearance. In fact, Crase's poetry had encomia lined up even before its publication. Jacket puffs were received from, amongst others, John Ashbery, Harold Bloom, Anthony Hecht, John Hollander and James Merrill; puffs which the publisher 'forgot', apparently, to publish on the dust jacket of the original hardback, although Ashbery, Hollander and Merrill did make it to the back cover of the paperback.

And the praise didn't stop there. David Kalstone, introducing Crase at a reading with Ashbery, commented, 'I think I speak for many in saying [*The Revisionist*] appeared with that sense of completeness of utterance and identity that must have come with the first books of Wallace Stevens – *Harmonium* – and Elizabeth Bishop – *North and South*'; Richard Howard in *The Nation* named it as one of his Books of the Year, calling *The Revisionist*, 'The most interesting book of first poems in many years'. William H. Pritchard wrote, 'This seems to me the voice of a potentially major talent, but certainly, at the least, that of a rewarding and original new poet.' Richard Tillinghast, David Lehman and Jay Parini also lined up to lavish praise. There were, however, dissenting voices: Louis Simpson objected to 'verbosity, and Crase is verbose. And he uses abstract language so that his argument is obscure – and he is always arguing'. William Logan described the poems as 'prosy... their movements similar, their tone bleached, do not have the variety that would differentiate one argument from another, one line from its peers', whilst suggesting that, 'Despite these flaws, the poems have a welcome intelligence and a force that suggests Crase may become a convincing topographer of "the beauty of something beautiful".' In reaching for kind of origin to Crase's style and subject matter, other critics looked to Whitman and Emerson, whose essays, Crase himself, has introduced for the Library of America.

In the search for Crase's poetic origins, an immediate reference point was Ashbery, and Crase was added to the 'New York School of Poets'. Harold Bloom saw Crase writing 'in the idiom of Ashbery'. Frederick Garber in *American Poetry Review* found 'a laid-back quality in Crase, a cool reminiscent of Ashbery in many of his modes, and, for this reader, of the early Miles Davis'. In his *History of Modern Poetry*, David Perkins comments that in *The Revisionist*, '[Crase] has absorbed Ashbery. I am thinking of Crase's bland tone, his occasional deliberate vagueness as to who is addressed or what is referred to, the clear, even intelligence of his writing which is continually observant, thoughtfully generalising, mildly witty, and at the same time, comfortable, friendly and low-keyed'. The connection to the New York School was further reemphasised in that James Schuyler's poem, 'Dining Out with Doug and Frank' refers to Crase and his husband, Frank Polach. David Perkins goes on to suggest that, 'Crase's subject matter [is] American history as it is reflected in particular places' but that 'the deeper meaning of his poetry lies in his vision of process, of unresting, somehow orderly change in natural things and also in buildings, cities or "history".'

Orderly change is, I would suggest, not quite what we get at the beginning of Crase's first book. *The Revisionist* opens with the title poem stating, 'If I could raise rivers, I'd raise them / Across the mantle of your past: old headwaters / Stolen, oxbows high and dry while new ones form, / A sediment of history rearranged.' These statements seem somewhat more than revision; more like wholesale uprooting and, as the text notes, 'rearranging'. And this sense of a massive violence wished up on the Other continues, 'If I had glaciers, / I'd carve at the stony cliffs of your belief; / Logical mountains lowered notch by notch, erratics / Dropped for you to stumble upon.' There are a range of techniques being brought to bear in all this. Firstly, there is the to and fro between the 'I' narrator and the 'you' who is the recipient, who is both 'America' and unnamed lover, assimilating both landscape and personality. Thus the 'you' has a 'mantle', 'headwaters', 'oxbows', 'cliffs', and 'mountains'. But these geographical and geological features also contain aspects

of personality: the mantle is 'the mantle of your past'; the sediment is 'a sediment of history'. Cliffs are 'stony cliffs of belief'; mountains are 'logical mountains'. These latter are interrupted by dropping 'erratics' upon them.

Such assimilation of place and personality might allow Crase to place himself into the tradition he announces in his introduction to his 'common-place' book, *AMERIFIL.TXT*.; 'a tradition by which the Americas themselves are the greatest poem'. Crase sees writers in this tradition of America as poem as 'poets we know as naturalists instead'. One such of these would be Aldo Leopold, the author of *A Sand County Almanac,* referenced in Crase's essay on Lorine Neidecker. But Crase is also nodding, perhaps, towards Emerson and his great essay, 'Nature', which, written in the Romantic era, almost inevitably moves into an engagement with the 'sublime':

> There are all degrees of natural influence, from these quarantine powers of nature, up to her dearest and gravest ministrations to the imagination and the soul. There is the bucket of cold water from the spring, the wood-fire to which the chilled traveller rushes for safety, and there is the sublime moral of autumn and of noon.

Here, nature is healing and nurturing. Yet, since Emerson's eyes look to nature as a vision of God, '[Nature] is loved as the city of God, although, or rather because there is no citizen', nature is sublime because it is unsullied; it is pre-lapsarian. And when humanity comes on the scene, when nature is moralised, that moralisation creates time, where humanity is subservient to the greater rhythms of nature. Frederick Garber also sees Crase's project in this light, 'What [Crase] sees in [the past] most of all is the plenitude of potentiality, knowing as he does that what occurs is the smallest slice of what could have happened. It is, perhaps, this sense of potentiality which is moralised for Crase; the potential for good or ill, and the indecisions and uncertainties which either creates for America.' This sense of potentiality complicates any idea that Crase is simply a painter of 'paysage moralisé'. As we have seen, Crase's tendency to address the landscape in the second person overlays the human and the landscape in Crase's ethics. And as we will explore later, such overlaying also shows Crase's environmental concerns in a way which 'paysage moralisé' would bleach out.

Crase develops these ideas in his long essay on Lorine Niedecker's poem, 'Lake Superior'; a poem he sees as springing from:

> a tradition that seems peculiarly American: it's a tradition we honor only partway. For the truth is, when our poets start telling us about gneiss, or land and air, when they locate their story in stone or, as Niedecker does, in rock, I think we allow them the trope but are not likely to believe they are saying what in fact they just said. They and their poems are made of land and air and rock. People who read poetry have always been alert enough to entertain the trope while avoiding the notion itself as sentimental, romantic, or worse, perniciously near to nationalism.

Or, as Crase puts it in his poem 'The Lake Effect': 'It's not that visibility / Is poor but that so much so visible must be perceived / Vastly obscure.' Crase clearly winces at the way the American landscape can be 'politicised', or at the very least viewed as having some message other than itself. What is reported by American writers to be seen in the American landscape may be both obscure and disbelieved. The Americas might be their own greatest poem, but to articulate that in poetry is immediately to populate it and thereby to compromise it. This sense of what such a compromise might mean was picked up by Stephen Burt some twenty years after the publication of *The Revisionist*. Writing about Crase's poem 'There is No Real Peace in the World', Burt comments:

> Crase's poem does not pretend that its uncertainties themselves amount to liberal politics: the privacies it investigates and the style it finds for them, grow from Crase's sense that against the fact of death in general, and the threat to America in particular, he cannot feel that he already knows what to do... Crase's poem suggests ways of thinking about impending catastrophe that appeal precisely because they are *not* ways of thinking that claim to speak for a community, nor to advocate a course of public action.

If America is its greatest poem then it is great in its multifariousness and potential depth of responses. Crase does not need to make America great again because its greatness is imbued in its ongoing potential; and if there is the potential for ill, it is a potential manipulated by those who would narrow, constrain and fix. For Crase, both the perception and the recording of it, the phenomenology, are provisional and inherently compromised, as he notes in 'The Revisionist', 'What I am after to remember is not what was, / and what I am anxious to save is not the same / For in the moment I saw you, you were changed.' The enterprise of the poem is endangered in the very moment of its conception.

Crase's use of 'you' in 'The Revisionist' allows America to be 'land and air and rock', but also to be a kind of Audenesque lover. And such a combination does actually allow the writer and the reader to distance themselves a little from the rearrangement. Well, perhaps it allows the European reader to distance themselves; the American reader might feel pulled into the poem as both creating and colluding in the aspects of personality the 'I' wishes to change; and to be part of that wincing compromise. At the end of the first section of 'The Revisionist', however, the 'I' admits their own needs, 'If I could unroll a winter of time / When these were done, I'd lay around your feet / In endless field where you could enter and belong, / A place returning and a place to turn to whole.' The narrator envisages himself lying at the feet of the 'you', 'when these were done.' The changes occur after a 'winter of time', and allow an 'endless field'; a field not only capable of nurturing, but with an Eliot-like sense of the place returning with a sense of accomplished wholeness.

Crase begins his sentence with 'If', and later in the poem he comments, 'In every district where there is / Restitution owing, where your riches inspired plunder / Instead of care, my outrage gathers on your interests / To give them form.' Where the poet seeks to express the interests of others, the response is likely to be conditional, emotionally etiolated, partial and mediated. This conditional and mediated agency is replicated in the way varying kinds of invasive species have colonised North America:

Loosestrife, the purple filler
At the low end of the field, came vagabonding
In the wool of distant English sheep and docked
At a Hudson river factory and now the Japanese
Lady's Thumb, having arrived as a stowaway
With the china, packed in straw, is deftly
Fulfilling its version of manifest destiny.

For Emerson, this 'uneasiness which the thought of our helplessness in the chain of causes occasions us, results from looking too much at one condition of nature, namely, Motion'. And, 'The reality is more excellent than the report,' as Crase himself quotes. Such uneasiness and helplessness are part of a set of contradictions from which 'the only way out is the sublime'. For Crase, the sublime embodied in Lorine Niedecker's writing is, 'the identifiable, continuing attitude of the tradition we should call, not the egotistical, but the evolutional sublime'. If this is Crase sidestepping Emerson, where 'evolutional' might imply 'Motion'; this implication is, perhaps, because Crase lives in the second half of the twentieth century, first part of the twenty-first. Crase lives in a post-industrial, post-*Silent Spring* world where process and motion are the ways an identifiable, continuing attitude to that natural world shows itself. Where Crase rejects an attitude that is 'sentimental, romantic, or worse, perniciously near nationalism', he, like Niedecker 'will not let [the] excursion into its sublime end in mere grandeur'.

Thus, Crase invests in a provisional phenomenology, 'For in the moment I saw you, you were changed.' When, as we have seen, Crase steps away from the politicised landscape, the landscape recorded and thus compromised, the answer is not simply to live in a changing world, a world which is rolling away from its location even in the moment of its being found; this is a world which is both 'being' and 'becoming'. The job of the poet is to record both these things. As Crase puts it in the poem, 'The Elegy for New York', 'I arrived in the visible city to look for you / where "time becomes visible with shape", as someone said. / With *shape*?' (Crase's italics). If time becomes visible in shape, then the shape is the crystallisation, the final 'being'. And the italicisation of 'shape', plays on the sense of finality, where the narrator questions the notion that time, or becoming, is concretised in that way; as if neither time nor the actual buildings of New York can be finalised. This is a poem which begins by showing how real estate is mutable and subject to monetary whim, '...the tick of property which can always assemble / to a bid. The air rights fidget about the vents, / Zoning and setback line up to be invested in'. In a Trumpian world, this depiction feels even more authentic. That definite article in the title, also seems to ironise its own existence as the definitive elegy for New York.

If a poet like Lorine Niedecker tries to reach through to the sense of being in the landscape, then she is automatically caught up in the notion of becoming, whether she wants to be caught up in that or not. Emerson might lament this as viewing nature from the single perspective of 'motion'; but Emerson's search for the sublime, needs reorienting, 'rearranging'.

One of Crase's responses to this sense of change and how it intends us and we intend it, is to examine the interior as manifested in the 'domestic'. For Crase, the domestic was a conflicted response to 'that innocent thesis *The Frontier*'. In 'America Began in Houses', Crase begins by stating, 'Unlike the other countries, this one / Begins in houses, specific houses, and the upstairs room / Where constitutions vibrate in the blockfront drawers / A Queen Anne Highboy'. What is noticeable here is how the poem begins with this short line containing the definite article and the phrase 'this one'. Thus America, although not named, is pulled into relation with 'the' other countries and then pulled into itself with 'this one', and those dynamics are held in the short line which re-emphasises them. In addition, 'Begins' is placed at the start of the line with further, almost mimetic, emphasis. For Crase, however, much of this sense of creating '<u>a home</u>' remains held in relation to 'home', the country of origin, from which the pioneer waited for news of 'the latest politics / From home: so much for that innocent thesis *The Frontier*'. The relation of 'a home' and 'home', becomes doubled in Crase's poem into a relation between 'artifice' and 'artifact'; and when this occurs, 'a national monument / is declared, but to visit it afterward is invariably / To be dismayed: could they have really planted lilacs / by the door'. This knowing reference to Whitman's 'When Lilacs Last in the Dooryard Bloom'd', Whitman's oblique elegy to Lincoln, suggests that both nation building and home building can be analogous, interwoven and fraught with complications. Both the monument and the elegy emerge out of these complications and signal the contingent stages in the process of creating a 'home', and its manifestation in a domestic landscape.

If a house is 'a carapace of a soul... / [then it is] not always of the occupant any more than the shell / of a hermit crab can be said to be his own'. The house or nation may not represent the soul of the occupant/people. That house or nation may 'take / some growing into, or making over'. The 'pilgrim aspirations' with their 'borrowed fashions' might evolve into a 'suburban mutant enlarging / nature once again'. Here, 'nature' has both the material sense of the world which the suburbs might create, but 'nature' is also the sense of attitudes, emotions and personality. The evolution is both inner and developmental, but also outer, visible and constituted.

In 'Lines from London Terrace', the title essay from Crase's 2017 collection of essays, Crase defines the '*evolutional* imperative' as, 'So act, and so write, that the rule by which you operate could be adopted universally without obstructing the process of evolution.' In fact, 'Lines from London Terrace' is a collection of diary entries from Crase's notebooks from the first half of 1987. Although these diary entries might be written 'on the hoof', Crase has chosen to concretise them in a book with their title as its title. It is possible that Crase might want to ameliorate such idealism, and such *ambition,* as we move further into the twenty-first century. And Stephen Burt feeling for the provisionality of Crase's poetry might want to argue that idealism is not, actually, Crase's real intention. However, when Crase uses the term 'evolutional sublime' about Lorine Neidecker's poetry, he defines it as 'a passionate deference to the organic and inorganic commonwealth that cannot otherwise speak for itself,' that sense then of the poetry itself as 'land and air and rock'.

Crase's own essay on John Ashbery 'The Prophetic Ashbery' is not collected in *Lines from London Terrace.* The Ashbery which Crase presents there is at once both commodious and available. In refuting Ashbery's reputation as 'private' and 'inaccessible', Crase maintains that 'Ashbery is most ruthlessly available to the present in our time' a present 'largely to be found in the curricula of the city and its sophisticated outposts'. Ashbery is the poet who has spent large parts of his life in New York, or Paris, and who has become part, some might say the locus, of much of the cultural life of those cities. As Crase puts it, 'When you put his capacity for taking in boarders together with the timely milieus in which the man has moved, the result is a brilliant, and thus dense, mingling of attitudes and their languages.' If Crase is perceived to be 'Ashbery-lite', then part of that 'lite' is that Crase has ploughed a narrower furrow. Although Crase can write with brilliant perception about Art, and about artifacts – few poets have written so well about furniture and furnishings! – Ashbery's simultaneity, as Crase puts it, is not part of Crase's poetic tool kit. And, I would venture, neither would he want it. Ashbery might provide an impetus into the poetry, but, as we have seen, it is the landscape and the possibility of America as its own greatest poem which is the subject matter of Crase's art. Crase's locates Ashbery within a city also evolving with its own urban identity and tradition, 'To the extent that the city includes the past, it is alive with all the suggestions of our culture' and Crase quotes from Ashbery's 'Self Portrait in a Convex Mirror, 'Rome where Francesco / Was at work during the Sack... / Vienna where the painting is today... / New York / Where I am now, which is a logarithm / Of other cities'. Thus Parmigianino's masterpiece provides one strand of evolutionary behaviour connecting urban life; the painting is an example of a meme of art making and curating which moves through cities. And that meme spreads into the sense of New York, itself, as an exemplar, perhaps, *the* exemplar/logarithm of urban living. Here, Ashbery is an exemplar of American culture at its best commodious and at pains not to claim to speak for particular communities or advocate public action.

The poems in Crase's chapbook, *The Astropastorals,* published in 2017 may seem a long way from the earlier world of blockfront drawers and Queen Anne highboys contained in *The Revisionist.* The opening poem, 'Once the sole province' continues, '... of genius here at home, / Was it this, our idea of access to a larger world / That invented the world itself (first, second, / Third) past accuracy we are bound to inhabit now / As targets'. Below, Crase continues, 'For we are either ready or / We must be ready or not, an expensive mix / of life-based chemistry perpetually on the verge / Of going to heaven in a vapor, and almost making it'. Here 'that innocent thesis *The Frontier*', is still a frontier but it is no longer so innocent. For Crase, God has not only absconded, but is an 'old outside agitator... who pump[s] the world with promises / Are simply not to be believed.' The promises of what we might achieve here on Earth spiritually and morally have failed to materialise. So the new frontier of space travel is a response to an urge to move beyond ourselves and access a larger world, 'So / Pity the day, beyond which we can see, / For if time is distance then distance must be life / And who is there on earth who will not go / In answer to its call?' This call which is 'The aim of every reverence.' [Ed: Correct?] However, even as Crase's diction feels so rhetorical, he seems to suggest that, actually, *not* everyone will 'answer to its call'. There are actually other kinds of reverence. As Perkins notes, there is the way in which, in the earlier poems, Crase's imagination invests the situation with the process of the imagination of that time, which may orientate towards an idealised, contemporaneous 'home' which has its own politics, its own imagined set of negotiated power relations. If *The Frontier* with its capital letters and italics could only be ironically 'innocent', *The Astropastorals*'s 'Once the Sole Province' contains similar ironies. Its future worlds are also the products of a 'genius at home'. This genius here at home has pushed into other worlds 'as targets'; targets in both senses here: targets of planetary exploration, but also targets in themselves, targets of the attacks of others, as the pioneers saw themselves as targets of 'Indians'.

If Perkins is correct, then Crase's view of the human process is one which moves towards and away from safety 'perpetually on the verge'; a projection of humanity's impulses for both home making and home threatening, particularly the 'home' of the Other. As Crase puts it in the poem 'Dog Star Sale', 'All involved on the earth with your chores of pollution / And likely never to pause / Let alone practice what we/ Observe: as far as you touch / Other worlds, that much you save yours'. Crase seeks to observe 'other worlds' and implores us to preserve them. *The Astropastorals* might play on both the idea of pastoral poetry by presenting a heavily ironised, interplanetary idyll, which 'meets their needs in scale: shops, / Ammo dumps, taverns and houses of prayer' ('Theme Park'). But there is also the sense of these pieces as pastoral letters, again speaking to the spiritual needs of those who inhabit the future. If both these kinds of pastorals are ironised, then Crase seems to suggest that we have to work harder at preserving what we have, not so much 'astropastorals' as 'anti-astropastorals'.

The Revisionist appeared in 1981. As Crase notes in *Lines from London Terrace*, that was a time when many of his friends were succumbing to AIDS. Although it was still a world which lived with the legacy of the Vietnam war, it was the beginning of the Reagan era. It might be too easy to say that *The Revisionist* spoke to the zeitgeist. But the poems in the book particularised an American experience which resonated with readers and critics who had grown up in a post-war period of rapid material and spiritual change. In 'Lines from London Terrace', Crase seems to characterise this as, 'They say hyperbole is when the language strains against the realities that constrain us: every time I, for instance, return my argument to "America"'. It is clear that for many of Crase's readers at that time, Crase was not guilty of 'hyperbole', neither did his language strain against reality. If Crase's argument was 'America', the detail and elegance of his writing means that the poems are never simply argument but are a way of elucidating and articulating a realisable, if constantly mutable, experience.

Four Poems

PARWANA FAYYAZ

A Letter to *Flower* and *Crown*

In the middle of the night,
I write a letter to *Bibi Gul* and *Taj Begum* imagining their daytrip.
Measuring the hours with the gesture of the sun,
they now cross the muddy valleys –

with a hope that someone will help on the other side,
offering them shelter to rest for the night.
I first heard the story about the women fleeing
and losing their ways in crossing the valleys –

to an end uninvited.
The reason for their flight remains a mystery,
and never to be remembered again.
The remaining people call their flight

an escape out of the village
in search of some distant land,
abhorrence, translates the word on the tip of the tongue.
Among those women were my two

great aunts, *Bibi Gul* Lady Flower and *Taj Begum* Madam Crown –
whom I did not know until one day I heard
my grandfather *Chaman* Grass curses them under his breath
'oh the creators of this twirling restless pain under my rib-bones... *Jankan Jankan*'

In his soulless echoes,
he named them *Siya Ru* the dishonored.
His pain grew deeper after his sisters were captured mid-way to the valleys
and were brought back and scorned by a hundred village men.

Later those women were sealed in the city-prison for disloyalty.
Women without men became pregnant in the prison –
giving birth to illicit children.
No names. No stories.

No past to be remembered.
Their children grew into complete humans,
scorning themselves for their anonymous fathers
and dishonoured mothers, who remained unknown to us.

I know they prepared for their losses –
fading in like echoes deep into the twirling valleys,
low heads and tired fingers to object.
To the lost women,

the village-men may never recall their return,
or may never tell the truth about
their lives in the harshness of the village-life,
so ready to chase away the white wolves of winters.

Here I measure time in the motion of my feet
crossing the oceans, to write their names,
and to find the knot that binds me to *Flower* and *Crown's* souls –
to give them names so they can rest for the night on their next escape.

Grandma's Old Love Story

On dinner *sofra*, girls are grapes
boys are pomegranates

I remember when I was a loving wife
your grandfather was as handsome as Joseph
I dream of him –
he wears his white shirt – young as the new apple blossoms

he calls for me
I am outside, the glow of the morning breezes –
I pick the last fresh tomatoes from the garden. I hear him calling me
I run toward him and see his handsome face...

A break in the conversation –

What was I saying
It was a beautiful thought

I felt I was drinking *taza* water –
from the well near the apricot tree
and felt my young lips kissing the air around the edges of the glass
What was that thing I was telling you

She remains silent for a longer time –
reflecting what
she had in mind that made her feel young again.
I dare not remind her.

Rain stops dripping now,

summer dryness enters the room,
and thirst overwhelms her.

She wants to go to the well to drink *taza* water –
with her weak knees, she pushes herself and crawls toward the stairs.
        Then I must go to the farms,
She now reaches the stairs.

The well was not there, I said.
'It was in the grand house of yours,
and we are not there anymore.'
The well. The husband. The young time. The dreams.

The tomatoes. And her thirst is forty years in the past.

Her mouth is now half-open,
the imprints of her age point around her toothless mouth.

She is trying very hard to weep.
        But he calls for me
        I'm outside, I'm beautiful
        the glow of the morning breezes

and I pick the last fresh tomatoes from the garden
I hear him calling me
I run toward him and only see his handsome face...
she says it over and over,

until the sunset when everyone goes to sleep
and dreams bring him to her.

The City-Route

In 2005, we were one of the million Afghan refugee families returning from Pakistan and moving toward our city, Kabul, with a million hopes and dreams in our heads. Seven children with our mother and father, we packed the things we desperately needed and left our lodgings in Quetta, Pakistan. We took the three days' journey over the mountains weathered in echoes of horror and holiness. We envisioned our return and tried to describe it with words and textures, joy and pain. In our minds, it was the city-route of our dreams and it always ended with us reaching a line of turquoise water running through the heart of Kabul – the Kabul River. That's what it was once, at least it had been turquoise in my parents' stories.

Until we reached the river. It had turned into a ghostly opaque line of no water, no color, and the shore was nothing but dirt and opium extracts.

Day 1

At the start of our journey,
the far-away mountains were coated in dust, naked and exposed.
The route toward Kabul was through *Khaybar Pass* and *Zabul* –
where we stayed for our longest rest period.

We ate some dried cooked chicken legs, the skin
tasted like dry sand in the faraway hills.
Some strange looking travelers,
gave us boiled eggs and fresh cucumbers.

On the way, among the valleys and trucks,
the men wore black and hid their faces,
except their eyes, searching to see.
Their women and children hid in the back of the truck, not able to see.

Covered in black, we spent the night in a motel,
where every corner smelled of opium,
gunpowder, sweat, and women.
Scarier than a living hell was that place.

Outside was dark as the pit of an unending tunnel –
we dared not to look up for the stars,
they would bleed
 like we did inside with our open eyes.

Day 2

We were leaving for the city-route
in four hours.
Father didn't sleep the entire journey,
something he usually did so easily.

Our truck paved over the dusty ground –
the roads became wider toward noon,
pure beauty was being born in yellow clay
and the far away lonely trees were hazing under the dust-land.

On the way, among the valleys and trucks,
the men wore charcoal-black
and hid their faces, except their eyes,
searching to see.

We stayed the night in *Qalat*,
the hotel served plain rice and fresh *naan* bread.
The uninvited ants circled our table in perfect order, I counted
the large red ones – I encounter them still in dreams.

We drove toward Kabul with nowhere in between,
until the next day's sun started to rise above the city-route.
The glamourous morning-wind rose
and carried the unwanted dust, circling around the mulberry trees.

Day 3

We were finally feeling a little joy,
Kabul – here we come!
Until we came on an abandoned car
in the middle of an open road,

with four wide-open doors.
Six fat dead men in white had been dragged around.
Blood on their faces, drying blood on their robes
Blood on the route.

We had to see them, so we saw them nakedly.
We felt a gripping silence in our throats,
shaking in our hands,
and weakness in our toes.

The driver was clever enough
to lose nothing to the scene.
He took a careful turn, and passed by the car-scene.
Until we found the source of the rising-sun

larger than the car lost to sight.
In the not-so-far distance a majestic chain of mountains
appeared among the wastelands – filled with snow
and the feelings of coming home emerged in *Paghman* Mountains.

Day 4

The high mountains appeared like signposts,
their clustered rocks coated in snow
reaching for the skies.
Far away, behind the mountains the city awaited us.

With silence and reawakening memories
with welling tears and throbbing pain in our backs and feet –
we arrived to the city of *Kabul*.
That's what it became then. Our city.

On the streets, in the midst of the fruit-carts and trucks,
the men wore grey turbans,
their faces intense, tanned – their eyes
brighter than the sun, searching to see.

We ate kidney beans for our late lunch
at my grandparents' home
and saw the news about *Shaima Rezayee*
shot dead in her house in Kabul.

With the afternoon sun, my uncle drove us in his taxi
to a war-torn house in the north.
Mother made curtains, father bought candles,
I cooked steamed rice for dinner.

That night we looked at the stars –
indefinitely shinning,
all different sizes, from all corners,
the night-sky filled our stomach.

Now for ten years I visit Kabul
every May and June.
I sleep facing the moon toward the south, where the prayer-mat is folded,
exhaustion is in the air.

And toward the end of my journey
the city becomes involuntarily
and dangerously romantic.
That's when I leave – in the middle of a dusty day.

End of the Winter

1.

That winter ended on a Friday.
Down the hills,
the mud slid, opening little holes
to keep the water warm within,
and for the spring lilies to grow in colors.

I first encountered the little green surfaces
holding the water
like mountains holding the glaciers,
when I escaped my cousins' bullying,
and hid behind the bushes.

I told my mother about the clover I found,
she asked me to look for a clover leaf with four open lobes,
I never found one.
Until I was twenty-five, and I first encountered one
on a California hill.

2.

The next winter also ended on a Friday.
Down the hills,
in the little opened mud holes
instead of the warm water
the spring lilies grew yellow among the rocks.

I had found and counted
the shedding skins of the snakes –
folded and unfolded on the drying ground.
Ivory, Shiny and Fragile,
like the grown-ups' long nails.

I pulled them gently into a corner
and lined stones around them,
so that the snakes would leave us in peace
in case they came to search for,
and wished to re-enter their dead remains.

Their countless discarded skins
cloistered near the hollowing stream
that always scared me;
it ran through the heart of our village
and nourished the white wolves in other villages.

3.

The last winter also ended on a Friday.
Down the hills,
in the little opened mud holes
instead of the warm water –
solid rocks grew in number.

The countless dark marbles rock around the stream
hosted creatures from the crawling snakes
to the howling wolves.
Yet what amazed me most was
my young cousins swimming in the running stream.

They took off their dresses
and with their complete naked bodies
jumped into the cold-warming water.
I waited for them above the rocks,
and saw them crawling under the rocks

and disappeared in search of other village streams,
where the slippery surface of the marble
felt warmer.
I sat cross-legged waiting for a better view
of the streams streams running between the hills

and the uncountable sheep grazing under the rays.
My cousins never returned in the water,
like the snakes – they appeared among the rocks,
naked and exposed to the sun,
in search of their new skins, happy and satisfied.

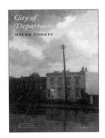

Hauntings

Helen Tookey, *City of Departures* (Carcanet) £9.99

Reviewed by PETER DAVIDSON

Helen Tookey has chosen a wholly apt image for the cover of this, her second collection from Carcanet: the mid-twentieth-century painter Algernon Newton's disquietingly motionless image of the Surrey canal at Camberwell. Small Georgian houses with dark windows, a lighted streetlamp, reflections, early evening clouds, empty air, no people:

> Canals have always seen too much.
> The blinded windows, the black
> thin trees – they swallow everything
> whole, show you precisely
> what they have taken.

This rich collection is pervaded by stillness, sadness, and disquiet and is much preoccupied with the poetic potential of twentieth-century painting. As well as a perfect evocation of the uncanniness of Newton's depopulated cityscapes, there are haunting considerations of the sparse twilight rooms and *rückenfiguren* of the Danish painter Vilhelm Hammershøi, and a sequence of poems whose sheer strangeness in dislocation of diction and object would seem to owe much to the Surrealists of the mid-century.

This second section of the book presents a series of disconnected voices reporting weird events and inexplicable transformations. There are visits to curious abandoned places which have once had a certain grandeur and are now in a state of menaced, very slow, metamorphosis. While remaining as elusive as they are beautiful, these verses seem to give a voice to the women depicted in the dream-pictures of surrealist painters: Leonora Carrington, Paul Delvaux, Leonor Fini. 'She brings you to the ponds, where the people are lying under the water. They are women, children, men – whole families.' Or

> [...] the drop from the patio
> down to the lawn, and all the way beyond
> to where she is, in the rose garden, staring
> at her right arm, its strange new blossoming.

The third section explores atmospheres of loss and alienation prompted by painting and writing of the first half of the European twentieth century. The focus is the world of Hammershøi's portraits and interiors – sombre enfilades of panelled rooms, the figures of his wife or sister, usually with their backs to the artist, or sitting motionless in front of the grey walls. In historical fact, these pictures depicted the interiors and effects created jointly by a visually-aware couple, experimenting happily with historicist and aesthetic effects in their spacious Copenhagen apartments. It is almost certain that they knew reproductions of paintings by the German Romantic Caspar David Friedrich, and that the series of paintings of women turned away from the viewer were a homage to the aesthetics of the early nineteenth century. But Helen Tookey transforms these works in imagination into compelling talismans of the sorrows of twentieth-century Europe: significantly, two 'Hammershøi' poems are placed on either side of the heartbroken 'What we can still do', a palimpsest of the letters of Ingeborg Bachmann and Paul Celan. The poem 'Strandgade (Ida Hammershøi)' is a distillation of loneliness, of time passing in silence with no communication between artist and model. 'Letter to Anna' imagines a sad future for the young woman in the portrait, a series of paragraphs from letters written to her in the comparative safety of Denmark from a close friend hoping to travel to join her, but unable to leave an un-named country on the brink of destruction in the conflicts of the twentieth century. This poem is an extraordinary achievement: it is a novel in five flawlessly cadenced paragraphs, a history of historical disaster and loving friendship, with the sad implication that the reunion hoped for in the last few words will never take place.

The volume concludes with a travel-dairy, a record of visits to Hammershoi's Copenhagen and of a journey down through Schleswig-Holstein to Hamburg and an exhibition of paintings by Anita Rée. It makes a perfect end to this finely ordered volume of verse which explores works of visual art as a way to open consideration of larger question of the arts and history.

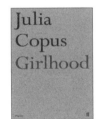

Forensic listening

Julia Copus, *Girlhood* (Faber) £14.99; Ilya Kaminsky, *Deaf Republic* (Faber) £10.99

Reviewed by HAL COASE

'Deafening silence.' Here is a phrase for the outraged, often used most publicly when *speaking out* is the just alternative. Its moral clarity depends on making two quick steps at once. 'The silence was deafening.' First, with its oxymoronic flare: the silence is so loud that I cannot hear anything. Second, a step back: I know what I should be hearing, I know what this silence is *not* saying – and so I hear exactly what it ought to say. 'We'd see the shadow of someone hitting, we'd hear the scream, then silence – suffocating silence.' These are the words of Mounir Fakir, then 39, when describing torture in Saydnaya Prison, the Syrian regime's mass execution centre. 'Suffocating', not 'deafening', perhaps because such horror leaves us without any idea of what should be said, what talk we should fill the silence with. In such a silence, you can't even breathe. Forensic Architecture, a research agency based at Goldsmiths, continue to make use of earwitness testimonies, such as Fakir's, to render models of the execution centre and describe what has happened there. They engage in what Lawrence Abu Hamdan, artist and collaborator on the project, has termed 'forensic listening'.

Ilya Kaminsky's *Deaf Republic* is forensic listening. It refuses, courageously, to be suffocated by the weight of its subjects. It attends to the power and powerlessness of silence, to what must be said and what must be left silent. It is unapologetically moral in articulating these distinctions and yet it knows exactly when ambivalence is called for. It knows that this is not an easy task. It is truly 'forensic' in its account of all these things. Every startlingly exact detail is evidence for violences that rip through the town of Vasenka – the fictional setting for a series of lyric poems presented in two acts, with *Dramatis Personae* given up front. But there is nothing distantly 'elsewhere' about these poems – their present tense feels all-encompassing. The frame, as the quotation marks around the '"we"' and the '"I"' in the character listings make apparent, is a way of drawing us in and insisting that the particular, when precisely rendered, can stand for the universal.

The collection's two acts recount the fate of Vasenka as it is occupied by soldiers. The soldiers kill a deaf boy watching a puppet show ('public assemblies are officially prohibited') and, in a miraculous response, the townsfolk become deaf. Kaminsky tears forward with this plot whilst circling back time and again to witness horrific acts with the vividness of war photography: 'Observe this moment / – how it convulses –'. There is a rich and expert play of form and style so that this sense of shocked 'convulsion' never leaves the page: long lines are pulled back suddenly to devastatingly short ones ('Ours is a country in which a boy shot by police lies on the pavements / for hours') and there is everywhere the literalism of violence threatening to overwhelm metaphor ('I, a body, adult male, awaits to / explode like a hand grenade'). This is poetry that interrogates its own ability to bear witness to violence without faltering in its belief that this must be its aim.

Kaminsky ends the collection with a brief note on silence: 'The deaf don't believe in silence. Silence is the invention of the hearing.' What such an invention could be used for troubles Julia Copus' poems in *Girlhood*, which have a moral clarity and linguistic force of their own. 'A Thing Once it is has Happened', with its broken rhythms, quotations and asides, and its slow unravelling of form, speaks on the page against the suffocating silence of trauma. There are poems here that dive into the gaps, the 'fissures', found within memories and archives, the spaces where silence is too often left to speak for itself. The collection concludes with a long sequence of dramatic monologues exchanged between Jacques Lacan and his most famous case study, Marguerite Pantaine, plus a 'chorus' of the inpatients in her psychiatric hospital. Copus is working here against the conspiracy of silence constructed around Pantaine: 'They worked in secret, almost out of earshot'. The clipped, clinical assessments of 'Lacan' are set against the rippling, densely woven interiority of his 'subject'. In her final monologue, 'Benediction', Pantaine escapes into an inner life beyond the reach of the doctors who impose their words on her:

But deaf his ears. Deaf
and always so, who is set to thinking
he has solved the puzzle of me. Good! And let him.

It is a complicated triumph, a kind of self-relinquishing release, but Copus is implacable throughout: violence is worth calling out for what it is. In *Mourning Becomes the Law*, Gillian Rose suggested that to argue for 'the witness of 'ineffability', that is, non-representability, is *to mystify something we dare not understand*, because we fear that it may be all too understandable, all too continuous with what we are – human, all too human.' In these two collections, there is a bold and far-sighted challenge to 'ineffability', along exactly these lines. They ask what fears might be hidden within deep silences. They find a polyphony of voices that are capable if not of dispelling these fears then at least of revealing how to use and how to break silence.

B*Witched

Rebecca Tamás, *Witch* (Penned in the Margins) £9.99

Reviewed by
BERNHARD FIELDSEND

I was reminded, partly, of Luca Guadagnino's film *Suspiria* when reading Rebecca Tamás's WITCH. Reminded then that witches recur in the imagination, and recently seem particularly present again; a character always available for reappraisal. The witch protagonist of Tamás's debut is multivalent: a geological being and an ecological effect, simultaneously global and local. Capable of existing both in and outside of time, she surveys human history whilst remaining ensnared by it. Among other things Tamás's book refracts climate change, feminism, pop-culture, philosophy, art, and the occult through this particular witch's eyes.

The book is dominated by two general types: The WITCH poems, and the *spells*. The former often have a casual, narrative style. Everything is heavily enjambed: rambling, repeating, meshing into itself. Tamás has a pleasing habit of rushing over images that other poets would cling to: 'a blue void of cloud cold planets shoals of birds', 'clean and sharp as an equation light slipping under chapped eyelids'. There is little time for pondering, the words keep coming: a stream of unpunctuated language is fired at the reader, spat even.

The *spell* poems are different, they open up space. A certain kind of artifice takes over in them. For me, they contain the most satisfying moments in the book, the kind of ambient noise they make becomes hypnotic. Fragments of 'friendly incomprehensible language' ('spell for exile') create a parallel world of associations, aligned but unseen:

then   somehow
as   much snow as you could ask for

wet-gold honey and locusts
   ('spell for reality')

The distinction between these two forms is not rigid. The writing styles mingle and infect one another, a *spell*-like moment in 'WITCH MARS' goes:

empty red dust   empress of a flat land cold boulders
sweet tender terrain of never - been - silt.

Much has been made of the corporeal and grotesque features of *WITCH*, little (I think) of its preoccupation with the slipperiness of knowledge:

If I say the witch knows things, you won't enjoy. I could smash every dousing crystal, apparition, rune, astrological symbol, bassinet, globe of silver, dagger, pleated skirt and we would still.
   ('Interrogation (2)')

In part, knowledge specific to women: of their historical selves, their future selves, their bodies, their collective experience. Not just the instinctive ownership of this knowledge, but the experience of doubting it too ('Witch Trials' makes heavy use of anaphora, with a repeating 'maybe'). In 'Witch Knowing' we encounter a strange being, 'a thing but not/ one thing', the tension of what it is/isn't in the poem is like the meeting of contradictory thoughts, a meeting which often forces us to recognise some uncomfortable internal hypocrisy. The confusion between knowing and not-knowing breeds this thing that is not one thing.

There are times when the scope of *WITCH* overwhelms its individual parts, but Tamás's commitment to her concept is consistently impressive. A forceful debut – I fear I've made it seem entirely serious, more often it is darkly humorous: 'you will menstruate exactly when the packet / tells you to' ('spell for logic').

Love and Otherness

Vidyan Ravinthiran, *The Million-Petalled Flower of Being Here* (Bloodaxe) £9.95

Reviewed by EDMUND PRESTWICH

The Million-Petalled Flower of Being Here is a sequence of a hundred loosely rhyming, metrically free sonnets written to his wife by a man of Sri Lankan Tamil ethnicity and heritage. In these days of polemical identity assertion it's refreshing to read a book whose explorations of identity and relationship are as generous, subtle and sensitively enquiring as these. No doubt this is because it's written out of love and the need to face the difficulties put in love's way by differences of ethnicity, gender, and the host of other factors that make us what we are. Two sonnets quote the opening phrase of Arcade Fire's 'My body is a cage'. Befitting his effort to escape the prison of self, Ravinthiran writes in a way that avoids the tendency of a dense, highly wrought sonnet to become cage-like, creating a field of force that folds inwards, enclosing whatever riches of thought and feeling it has within itself. That, it seems to me, is what the great stand-alone sonnet must do. But Ravinthiran hasn't written stand-alone sonnets, he's written a sequence whose beauty, growing with each rereading, depends on the reader's being drawn into the movement *between* poems, with its endless process of adjustment and discovery.

This way of writing involves sacrifice, as we see in the first poem:

I was reading my book by the window
waiting for you when I noticed one flower
of those you'd artfully splayed had snapped.
Like a limp wrist the orange gerbera hung, and over
my knuckle it vented a beige gunge. As I snipped
the stem for a smaller vase, the glow
of the radiant petals was too much. Time lapped
me round, the day went unseized.
For this was no opportunity I could have missed;
only the lonely moment which blazed
in my hand unplucked. Like many
I had forgotten that time isn't money
and I don't need always to be on the move
within the world you've shown me how to love.

There's a self-contained beauty to the way the sudden blazing of the moment is described, but in a sense the essential life of the poem is in the weaker lines at beginning and end. They give the momentary illumination its meaning as part of the ongoing story. In themselves, the last two lines are facile and sentimental. After reading the whole book, you see them as a first stab at expressing something that can never be bluntly said, only lived through and expressed in concrete detail.

An incidental pleasure of the book is the recognition of a multitude of quotations, including whole found sonnets that strike a chord with elements of the story of Ravinthiran's love and its obstacles. Brief allusions may playfully subvert their original contexts, like the quotation from Eliot's 'Ash Wednesday' in 'Aubade', or may open ambiguous vistas of suggestion, like the echo of Muldoon's 'Wind and Tree' in the same poem. Such pleasure is a bonus. The heart of the volume is the thoughtfulness with which personal difficulties are related to wider issues, the intimacy with which personal vulnerabilities are revealed, the radiance of the love breaking through clouds of difficulty and distraction, and the generosity of spirit looking with an equal eye at the poet's own experience and that of other people. In this way, I particularly liked 'She', about the poet's cousin's wife joyously surmounting the difficulties of immigrant life in Canada: 'to be fearless and immediate / in a strange, cold country means giving birth / to oneself every day – and with every breath.'

Cinematic Shopping List

Laura Scott, *So Many Rooms* (Carcanet) £9.99

Reviewed by
JOE CARRICK-VARTY

Many of my favourite poems in *So Many Rooms* deploy sequences and instructions. Essentially they are list poems comprised of keenly observed and, more importantly, intricate calls-to-action, as in 'Buster Keaton', a stunningly short and transformative twelve-liner: 'Find a stone that reminds you of the moon./Hold it in your hand until it becomes a face'. The key to a great list poem is intrigue. Without intrigue the list reads like, you guessed it, a shopping list, of eggs and cheese and milk, not a poem in which images are building, 'Blink away the colour from your eyes', piling up, 'see him flickering/in black and white', transposing between one and other, 'moving across the film/of your eye like bits of branch blown/across a dusty road' because this is what Scott's poems do so well, they sequence images of such veracity and subtlety, until, before we realise where we are, the house (and poem) is collapsing around us (and old Buster), 'blessing him with its open window.' And the reader, like our stuntman, gulps air once more. 'Buster Keaton' is a tiny poem. But already we see how far it reaches. How far it has come and, so typically of *So Many Rooms*, how far it will go – from stone to moon to face to hand to house – with Scott in the Director's Chair.

Typical of this cinematic quality are the collection's opening three *War and Peace* poems. 'If I could Write like Tolstoy' begins in filmic realism, with Scott on set, literally talking to us through a megaphone: 'you'd see a man/ dying in a field'. A narrative web unfolds with a kind of effortless, even careless sparseness: 'I'd take you close until you saw the grass/blowing around his head'. Scott zooms in, zooms out, refocuses: 'I'd show you/a pale-faced Tsar on a horse under a tree,/breath from its nostrils... perhaps hoofmarks in the mud'. This 'perhaps' is key to the kind of perpetuity these poems generate. Despite Scott's instructional tone, the poems evolve as if by accident: 'You'd hear ice crack', terrible accident, 'You'd feel/ the blood coming out of the back of someone's head'.

A poet friend Rowland Bagnall once said to me, imagine a narrative as a lake – the bed of the lake where water ends, where light ends, where the bigger fish lurk, and then the top of the lake where sky opens up with birds, sun etc. You get the picture: many endings, many beginnings, all that distance in between. What Laura Scott does is she walks to the lake, cups her hands, and offers a sip of water each time. A snapshot of a massive, looming, living lake of story which, nonetheless, echoes and echoes. And then a final admission, a wonderful and guiltless parting admission:

Then I'd make you wait – for pages and pages –
before you saw him, go to his window

and look at how the moon turns half a row
of trees silver, the other half black.

Rest in Motion

John Wilkinson, *My Reef My Manifest Array* (Carcanet) £12.99;
John Wilkinson, *Lyric in Its Times* (Bloomsbury Academic) £90

Reviewed by IAN BRINTON

The thirty-three poems of the sequence 'Bodrugan's Leap' form the central section of John Wilkinson's most recent publication of his poetry. The title of the sequence refers to a moment in 1487 when Sir Henry Bodrugan, pursued for treason, leapt from a Cornish clifftop into a waiting boat that took him to France. As we are informed on the back cover, the totemic image of exile 'feeds an interest in borders and partings that runs through the collection'.

Language stands at the threshold of visibility and words are themselves a leap into space. Just as we end at our skin, encased in mortality, our words are thrust out into air, a lyric pulse where 'vacancy overcomes these ruses of / navigation'. Words in John Wilkinson's poetry,

jump from broken turf to where a dinghy
writhes on shoulders
of a deep-dyed
but trustworthy sea, a boat that shudders,

tense for his plunging onto its thin planks –

It is in the ten chapters of *Lyric in Its Times*, which had begun life as a group of essays and a seminar series about lyric poems as objects and events, that Wilkinson reminds us of another jumping 'from broken turf' with the poetic and visual tradition of metamorphosis haunting the Western tradition: transformations from human to stone, tree, plant or animal. These words in turn bring to mind those of the critic Jeremy Noel-Tod when he reviewed an earlier Wilkinson collection, *Lake Shore Drive*, for *The Guardian* over ten years ago. Noting how Wilkinson's poems bring 'familiar words into an unfamiliar synthesis' he recognized how multiple lines of thought cross and knot in a worldwide web 'corded with lines of flight".

Lyric in Its Times is subtitled 'Temporalities in Verse, Breath and Stone' and the generous wealth of close analysis looks at lyrical poetry from Shakespeare to Shelley, from Baudelaire to Prynne. Examining the tracks left by travelers in Prynne's end of the century sequence *Triodes* Wilkinson notes the trade relations of the sugar industry revealing what he calls the 'grammar of brute exploitation' which, as readers, we view from our balcony seats. As we also do when we watch the 'arrows / of a plotted course' in 'Bodrugan's Leap'.

The lyric poet opens doors and the poetry of John Wilkinson gazes through gates, gaps, stone cromlechs and the eye, itself a window to the soul, reflects Janus-like upon the self through its study of intricacy of form in both language and the natural world. Referring to both Andrew Crozier's last published poem, 'Blank Misgivings', and Philip Larkin's farewell to the cliff's edge in 'Aubade' Wilkinson refers to the lyric in action: 'Stones fall and rest at once, they are in motion and settled. The simplest words come to rest in motion.' Words, like stones, are a testament to what has taken place and Wilkinson alerts us to the way in which the Larkin poem voraciously drags us into 'its death vortex' as contrasted with Crozier's 'Blank Misgivings' in which 'The ruined landscape fills with sounds and obstructions'. Larkin's poem exists 'so as to assert the end of hermaneutics' whereas Crozier's poem asserts a ruined landscape which is filled with 'sounds and obstructions'; Crozier's poem is 'haunted by futurity as well as the past'. Words like stones remain jutting up through landscapes.

The image of a traveler haunts *My Reef My Manifest Array* and the titles of John Wilkinson's poems reflect aspects of the journey: 'Down I Come', 'Facing Chesil Beach', 'So Far and No Further', 'Wapping Steps'. Monuments, the evidence of time passing, stand like henges opening up doors to a world which has been created by a lyric leap.

'Chysauster in Mist', the book's second section, opens with an epigraph from the Lebanese-American poet, Etel Adnan: 'Who are we, a race, a tribe, a herd, a passing phenomenon, or a traveler still travelling in order to find out who we are, and who we shall be?'

It is from this perspective that we are asked to view the late Iron Age and Romano-British village of courtyard houses which lies a few miles north of Penzance in the Penwith District of south-west Cornwall:

Moor swings out, travelers are taken on its liverwort
and furze along with scrawny horseflesh, shivering
like sun on racing water

The lines open on the run as it were and the fast movement of 'swings' is juxtaposed with the accuracy of identification of 'liverwort' and 'furze'. As the eye moves from the 'shivering' of the flanks of horses it traces its transience of vision in light which is in constant motion. The racing water has an echo of Heraclitean flux.

The third of the eleven poems in the Chysauster sequence opens with a surge of movement:

Fly to the border of convictions as if shape were but
their loss of traction, a disempowered glide, to shape
up meant to thicken

Winged movement to the edge at which insight becomes manifest is prelude to a leap, a glide, an idea of the future contained in the words we use. Macbeth recognized this when he referred to the approaching murder of Banquo in terms of 'Light thickens, / And the Crow makes Wing to th'Rookie Wood'.

The final chapter of *Lyric in Its Times* looks closely at an elegy titled 'The Thermal Stair' written by W.S. Graham 'For the painter Peter Lanyon killed in a gliding accident 1964'. The closing lines of the poem combine movement and stasis:

Uneasy, lovable man, give me your painting
Hand to steady me taking the word-road home.

As with Sir Henry Bodrugan's leap to freedom from the Cornish heights the death of Peter Lanyon prompts both Graham and, fifty years later, Wilkinson to wonder what is 'home' and the author of *Lyric in Its Times* concludes by heralding the 'repeatedly evanescent act of the poem which must wear a changeable, mortal disguise' in order to make 'poetic enlivening possible'. As James Joyce recognized in *Finnegans Wake*, the movement of words through air metamorphoses into printed stillness and the repetition of 'Shem and Shaun' will result in 'stem or stone'.

Poem Setting

Kalimba, Petero Kalulé
(Guillemot) £10

Reviewed by ANTHONY BARNETT

Petero Kalulé's poem 'Transcribing Noise', in three parts, *Compression*, *Amplitude*, *Rarefaction*, opens: 'listening presents itself as an everyday maintenance, twigwork'. I have a bee in my tree, my bonnet, a bee both calm and noisy, which is that composition lies at the heart of poetry while improvisation lies at the heart of music. That's rather simply and easily put and it leaves out a good deal of probably required explication but somehow I think Petero Kalulé might agree. I have written about this working theory of mine elsewhere so I won't labour the point again, except to say that I once toured with Douglas Oliver and his *Diagram Poems*, and musicians including Evan Parker, as Composed Poetry and Improvised Music. I was both: musically the percussionist. No, in no way was it that thing called poetry & jazz. I've touched critically on that too – with a little history about a different thing, the setting of poetry to music – in my monograph on Nancy Cunard's consort, *Listening for Henry Crowder*, and in 'True Musicians', which is an essay about the New York Art Quartet and Amira Baraka in *Antonyms Anew: Barbs & Loves*, as well as in a 1990s interview with D. S. Marriott, scion, in my book, of Aimé Césaire. Poetry & jazz, along with poetic offerings by jazz musicians, some of them truly great musicians: forget it, most of it. Agree or not, one could not do better than to look at many of the poems in Renate da Rin's anthology *Silent Solos: Improvisers Speak*, from her unprepossessingly named Buddy's Knife Jazzedition.
Petero Kalulé's debut collection *Kalimba*, whose format and cover are quite like the musical instrument of that name, also known as mbira, zanza, or in English, only so-so true, thumb piano, is another matter. Kalulé, who hails from Uganda, is completing a PhD in Law at Queen Mary University of London. But surely his heart lies elsewhere: in music and in poetry. He is a significant multi-instrumentalist, with alto saxophone to the fore – Guiseppi Logan is an inspiration – who performs dynamic improvisations which belie his gentle personal manner. While Kalulé's poetry is informed by musics, and dance, of all kinds – Cecil Taylor's dancing pianism

is one vital presence throughout *Kalimba*: 'dance hurtling Cecil' – it is also like a set of highly literary notations. (Allow that most of my quotations here do not take account of indents and spacings.) Kalulé has a penchant for such as '*s* oft' or 'ancient tXts' or, in 'Optics', 'y/our i lashes'. These are not gestures, as they might be in lesser hands, but part of a fully integrated, essential to his purpose, praxis. It is as if Kalulé wishes to squeeze every last drop of sense and sensitivity out of his letters, his syllables, his words. And he does.

'Collective noem' is the one poem not in English, and we may wonder at that:

> témû manyi, nti bano
> nabo éno néri babona
> > > bona
> nti fféna, mûno mûno mûnsi
> éno tûbonabona

while in the following poem 'Even': 'i whisper you in me' is three times repeated. 'Wounded Mangoes' opens: 'don't forget home, / he says / : your people, / your friends, / do not forget home'. Colloquial 'don't' changes to pressing 'do not'. There is compassion too. 'Rocking Chair': 'in the press of its leather / i am held / by his absence,', and in 'Memory is a sort of mother':

> now that she is O oldalone, mother's mother
> mostly talks about how she lost her mother
> > this is her comfort, little
> > else little else little else

Compassion but also a quiet anger. 'What we always мoᴎ' is an extraordinary evocation of childhood and subsequent discovery: 'what to do with that donation, / that gifted "*talent releasing*" piano', in which the instrument's ivories, unsurprisingly, take on other significances: 'we do not know / (for example) / that the whites / are displaced,' and 'we know not^e / that the ivories have paled / the elephants are extinct,'.

I am sure that this musician and poet understands full well the processes and implications of equivalence and difference in composition and improvisation. Petero Kalulé is a vital new force in our music and in our poetry, both passionate and unassuming.

In 'Cantabile – *rereading WCW*' 'here peeps a man / in / morning mist s enlace, st- / / ringing fiddle musics / / to / the rising peppers / in his garden'. And 'The truth' opens: 'how do you exit a poem? / you do- / n't, you / may walk out of it unsung, outsung'.

Winners, All

Warda Yassin, *Tea with Cardamom* (smith|doorstop) £5
Faith Lawrence, *Sleeping Through* (smith|doorstop) £7.50

Reviewed by RORY WATERMAN

With the proliferation of creative writing courses and workshops, and the democratisation of publishing, has come a bloated generation of new poets – some rather good, many awful. In addition to a near-simultaneous growth in the number of magazines and other outlets in which they might publish (or 'publish'), and the recent uptick in the number of small presses (the website *Sphinx* lists nearly one hundred active British poetry pamphlet publishers) there are now also more small prizes than ever catering for their hopes and, sometimes, expectations. Opportunity isn't a *bad* thing, of course, but where is a reader to begin to make sense of it all?

He or she might gravitate towards the prize-winners. The myriad and often well-documented problems with poetry prize culture, and what it means, have increasingly been augmented in recent years by that most enterprisingly American of practices: the poetry publication prize, often targeted at the new and eager. The hopeful masses send in their Word documents, and usually also their money; those fortunate enough to be picked off rebranded slush piles can be heralded on front covers as winners. The presses certainly win, not least because demonstrating that you nurture talent appeals to the Arts Council, a major source of potential revenue. But so do the chosen poets: it looks good to be a winner, and all but the no-hopers who help to keep the boats afloat might have their turns one day, somewhere. At the pamphlet press I run, New Walk Editions, we haven't succumbed to this model – but we can only publish four pamphlets a year, and never have any spare money. Surely if we changed tack, we could publish more poets we believe in. But a small fee can be a lot to some people, and the few aspiring poets left in garrets metaphorical and literal might be dissuaded. And what about the excellent not-new poets who have been pushed aside by this ever-replenishing trend for newness? It's complicated.

Smith Doorstop – AKA, and without irony, The Poetry Business – has recently operated three competitive schemes leading to publication, on various models, including the one so charitably outlined above. The focus is largely on 'exciting new voices', to coin a phrase, and in a world of 'exciting new voices' which are often, when it comes down to it, nothing of the sort, they've done a pretty good job at hoovering up more than their fair share of genuine talent. Their fees aren't astronomical: £28 for the International Book and Pamphlet Competition is perhaps a bit much for a glorified submission fee, but the New Poets Prize costs £8; the Laureate's Choice scheme is free, but then again it isn't open for submissions, so presumably it helps if you are known by the press – which happens to run frequent one-day workshops in the north of England, where most of their poets come from, for £35–£40 a go.

Warda Yassin is one of four winners of the New Poets Prize: those three words take up most of the front cover of *Tea with Cardamom*, just to make sure you know. She has an almost filmic gift for presenting a version of contemporary urban Britain:

> The breeze
>
> brings the Adaan, dubstep and sirens,
> the smell of the sauna, the smoke of incense.
>
> Out front, my father breaks his fast,
> chews dates, offers a cautious smile
>
> to those with heavy eyes across the way.

Yassin is a British-born Somali, and that heritage is at the heart of many of these poems – in sights, sounds, prayer:

> We stand in rows like soldiers there to learn the ways
> of the second life. *You can use whatever language you like.*
>
> *Hooyo, do not bow, there is only oath and dua between you
> and Allah, stay shoulder to shoulder with your sisters.*

Unsurprisingly, that heritage sometimes weighs heavy, and her debut is marked by consummately nuanced, reflexive poetry. This is mature writing, at once urgent and restrained. Some of her control comes from juxtapositions, and the complexities they can tacitly belie: 'When the war began, my aunt was detained between borders / like a pattern trapped under tapestry. // I love gold eye shadow and reading books about war.' 'I want to read a novel about Somalis that isn't trauma porn', she writes at the start of 'Tales', perhaps the finest poem here. We're then given a phantasmagorical montage, real and removed:

> We are not pirates, but mermaids lazing by crystalline
>   lagoons, shiid
> hoisted to the waist, buoyant youths swimming to jaamacad
>   in coral crowds,
> the rainforests of our sea. On the beach there is no blood,
>   only vendors
> reciting poetry, and there are no droughts on these dry pages,
>   turn a leaf
>
> and drift to the souk at dhur and see how we barter and flirt
>   in the baking hours [...].

For the Laureate's Choice scheme, four pamphlets a year are chosen for publication (but for some reason not introduced – perhaps she's too busy) by Carol Ann Duffy. As the new incumbent, Simon Armitage, is a local lad – Smith Doorstop is based in Sheffield – maybe we'll find out what his choices are next year. The most consistently impressive of the current crop is Faith Lawrence's debut, *Sleeping Through*, though each of the four has something to recommend it. Lawrence's are tight and precise poems – often extraordinarily so. The subject matter is largely conventional, but she writes intriguingly enough to startle. She is evidently a newish parent, and poets who are newish parents often fail to realise that what is life-altering for them isn't necessarily very interesting for anyone else; but here, the epiphanies can be as mind-shifting as

they can be cutesy, and don't outstay their welcomes. This is the entirety of 'Delivery':

> Baby, you took your time;
> nothing else was in the world
> until you found that ring
> of bone, and clever as a key
> you turned, slipped right
> through and unlocked me.

In the next poem, though, there is trepidation: 'all I can promise', she writes at the end of 'Summer Born', is 'a nest shaped to both / of us, somehow.' Notice the risk of fracture in that enjambment; notice the tension between 'promise' and 'somehow'. Lawrence is always attentive to such poetic and linguistic possibilities. All of these poems are this quick on their feet.

That isn't to say every move comes off. 'Flowering', a sequence 'after eleven paintings by Sophie Breakenridge', is pithy almost to the point of insubstantiality – and some advice on how to find the paintings might have been nice. But the pamphlet really comes alive again in the final section, with its subtly clever contradictions and interrogation of a huge theme in miniature. In 'Abduction', ostensibly about Persephone being seized and taken to the underworld, 'my heart was a bee in a half-closed fist'. In 'Afterlife', on the facing page, 'Heaven' is stifling, rose-tinted merriment, encapsulated in something reminiscent of a lifestyle magazine picture from early last century:

> a lido on the coast
> where the dead are playing catch
> in swimming costumes
> and flowery bathing caps [...].

'Quieting' gives a rather different version of the 'end of the world': it 'will not mean / more of everything // but less'. The pamphlet then ends with its shortest non-sequence poem, the three-line 'Gift': 'The gift of winter / is to limit us'. This could almost be taken as a metaphorical manifesto for this terse, urgent little body of work – which probably shouldn't retail for almost as much as a full collection, though that is a different matter.

In a culture of poetic bombast, quieter 'new voices' such as these two are likely to be drowned out. 'Exciting' needn't mean loud, unless that's all you are personally able to hear. So, whatever one feels about the brave new world of poetry publishing, Smith Doorstop deserves a lot of respect for giving these poets a platform.

Paul Muldoon is Howard G.B. Clark Professor in the Humanities at Princeton University. His thirteenth collection, *Frolic and Detour*, was published by Faber and Faber in September 2019. **Sujata's Bhatt**'s latest books from Carcanet are *Collected Poems* (PBS Special Commendation, 2013) and *Poppies in Translation* (PBS Recommendation, 2015). **William Poulos** is a poet and journalist. Among his many projects, he is researching Alexander Pope's engagement with Latin poetry. Follow him on Twitter @PoetryPoulos. **N. S. Thompson** is the non-fiction editor of *Able Muse*. He co-edited *A Modern Don Juan: Cantos for these Times* (2014) and his most recent poetry collection is *Mr Larkin on Photography and Other Poems* (2016). **Sean O'Brien**'s tenth book of poems, *It Says Here*, is to be published by Picador in spring 2020. It contains both a new collection and the book-length *Hammersmith*. He is Professor of Creative Writing at Newcastle University. **Yvonne Reddick** is the author of *Spikenard* (Laureate's Choice 2019), *Translating Mountains* (Seren 2017) and *Ted Hughes: Environmentalist and Eco-poet* (Palgrave, 2017). Her poems appear in *The Guardian* and *New Statesman*. **Wang Fang** is an English Language lecturer at Shanghai University of Sport. Her research focuses on the poetry of Robert Frost and Tao Yuanming. Her poetry translations from Mandarin are forthcoming in *Smoke* magazine. **Angela Leighton**'s latest publications are *Spills* (Carcanet 2016) and *Hearing Things: The Work of Sound in Literature* (Harvard 2018). **Andrew Wynn Owen** is a fellow of All Souls College, Oxford. He received the Newdigate Prize in 2014 and an Eric Gregory Award from the Society of Authors in 2015. *The Multiverse* was published by Carcanet in 2018. **John Gallas** is a New Zealand poet of eighteen, soon to be twenty, collections of poetry (mostly Carcanet), Orkney St Magnus Festival Poet, translator, librettist and Fellow of the English Association. **Kurt Gänzl** is the author of several standard works on music and theatre and of a series of biographies culminating in the 100-part 'Victorian Vocalists' (2017). **Iain Bamforth** lives in Strasbourg. His latest publication *Scattered Limbs: A Medical Dreambook*, a miscellany in which contemporary medicine confronts its origins in philosophy and mythology, is forthcoming from Galileo. **Ian Pople**'s *The Evidence* is published by Melos Press. **Hal Coase** is a playwright and poet. His most recent play, an adaptation of *Mrs Dalloway*, was staged at the Arcola Theatre last year. He lives in Bologna. **Joe Carrick-Varty** is an Irish/British poet who lives in London. His debut pamphlet *Somewhere Far* (The Poetry Business) won the 2018 New Poets Prize. He is a founding editor of *bath magg*. **Peter Davidson** is Senior Research Fellow of Campion Hall, Univeristy of Oxford. **Edmund Prestwich** grew up in South Africa. He taught English at the Manchester Grammar School for thirty-five years and has published two collections of poetry. **Ian Brinton** co-edits *Tears in the Fence* and *SNOW* and is closely involved with the Modern Poetry Archive at the University of Cambridge. His recent publications include a *festschrift for J.H. Prynne* and a translation of the selected poems of Mallarmé. **Parwana Fayyaz** is born in Kabul, Afghanistan is currently working towards a Ph.D. on the medieval Persian poet Jami at Trinity College, Cambridge. **Sinéad Morrissey** is the author of six collections, all published by Carcanet, and the recipient of both the T.S. Eliot Prize and the Forward Prize. She is Professor of Creative Writing at Newcastle University and Director of the Newcastle Centre for the Literary Arts. **Sarah Rothenberg** is a pianist and essayist who writes frequently on the intersections of music, literature and painting. She is artistic director of DACAMERA and lives in Houston and New York. **Bernhard Fieldsend** is from Wales. **Ned Denny**'s version of the *Divine Comedy*, *B: After Dante*, will be published by Carcanet in June 2020.

COLOPHON

Editors
Michael Schmidt
Andrew Latimer

Editorial address
The Editors at the address on the right. Manuscripts cannot be returned unless accompanied by a stamped addressed envelope or international reply coupon.

Trade distributors
NBN International
10 Thornbury Road
Plymouth PL6 7PP, UK
orders@nbninternational.com

Design
Typeset by Andrew Latimer
    in Arnhem Pro

Represented by
Compass IPS Ltd
Great West House
Great West Road, Brentford
TW8 9DF, UK
sales@compass-ips.london

Copyright
© 2019 Poetry Nation Review
All rights reserved
ISBN 978-1-78410-829-8
ISSN 0144-7076

Subscriptions (6 issues)
INDIVIDUALS (print and digital):
    £39.50; abroad £49
INSTITUTIONS (print only): £76;
    abroad £90
INSTITUTIONS (digital):
    subscriptions from Exact Editions
    (https://shop.exacteditions.com/
    gb/pn-review)
to: *PN Review*, Alliance House,
    30 Cross Street, Manchester
    M2 7AQ, UK

Supported by